ĐELAYED

BUT NOT DENIED

20 Inspirational Stories About
LIFE AND RESILIENCY

Compiled by
Toni Coleman Brown & Julia D. Shaw

DELAYED BUT NOT DENIED
20 Inspirational Stories About Life and Resiliency

Copyright © 2016, Toni Coleman-Brown, The Network for Women in Business.
Julia D. Shaw, Shaw Biz Consulting

Published by Quantum Leap Productions LLC
444 Beach 22nd Street
Far Rockaway, NY 11691

www.networkforwomeninbusiness.com
toni@networkforwomeninbusiness.com
www.shawbizconsulting.com
shawbizconsulting@gmail.com

ISBN 978-0-9787568-2-6

Published in the United States

Book cover and Inside Layout:
Karine St-Onge
www.shinyrocketdesign.com

ACKNOWLEDGEMENT

I want to take this time to thank every author who contributed to this project. This has to be one of the best book projects in which I have participated and compiled. Every story is priceless. Every author is unique and special in his or her right. Special thanks to my partner in good, Julia Shaw. Also thanks to Regina Finkelstein for her keen proofreading and editing skills. And a big thanks to Karine St-Onge of Shiny Rocket Design for her amazing skills. Also, I could not do what I do with the most High God, so all praises to Him. And finally, I want to give all my family members a big shout out, especially Sandy, Sasha, and Taylor.

Toni Coleman Brown

I want to thank God for my village of family, friends and co-authors. You helped build my character, making me wiser and stronger. I must acknowledge my queen mother Letha M. Shaw, she is the guiding star in my life; my sister Sherry and big baby brother Eddie; Asia Mya, Denisha Sher and all my princess daughters; Kamari, Destiny, Khloe and all my amazin grandchildren! A special thanks to Toni Coleman Brown! I love all ya'll!!

Julia D. Shaw aka "Julez"

TABLE OF CONTENTS

Compiled by **TONI COLEMAN BROWN** & **JULIA D. SHAW**

INTRODUCTION

This book is a vehicle, a triple-decker luxury bus traveling on the road of success fueled by the power of collaboration. "Delayed But Not Denied" is a vehicle of healing and transformation. We have given each of the co-authors a turn to drive and be at the wheel as we all travel together down the road of empowerment. Each co-author shared their bumps and potholes in the roads with the hope of helping readers of this book avoid the same obstacles they have endured. By chance, if any of the readers already hit the same potholes as our co-authors, they will know they were not alone and that there is sunlight at the end of the road.

Each co –author has stepped out on faith and joined us (Toni & Julia) on a journey of faith in action. What is really special about this book is the fact that every situation seems dire and murky in the beginning but turns into a triumph in the end. Each of the 20 authors appear on the surface to be unbruised, however, in each story they have taught us how to overcome with self-love and faith. We are encouraged by every story and know that you will be as well.

Our message to our readers is of resilience against the odds. Each one of the co-authors shared one of their many life-changing experiences with us. Their reasons for sharing their truth may vary. We recommend a specific method to read this book. And that is to reach each story from beginning to end and then journal about how it has impacted you and how you have been changed or encouraged by the author's body of work. This is the reason why we have blank pages in the back of the book.

We want you to journal and to express your truth. We also want to encourage you to begin the process of writing your own "Delayed But Not Denied" story. If you have experienced a situation and overcame it in a major way, then this may be just the opportunity for you. We would like to invite you to participate in our next book project, "Delayed But Not Denied: Volume 2."

If you're interested in participating in our next book project, please visit **www.delayedbutnotdenied.info** to discover how you can become a bestselling author in our next book. In the meantime, I hope that you're blessed by these stories as much as we have been.

As sisters in business, we both share the drive to grow and prosper as entrepreneurs. we are both driven to help others to succeed at their purpose and make their dreams of becoming bestselling authors come true.

Passionately,
Toni Coleman Brown & Julia D. Shaw

ABOUT
Melanie Turner-Kirkland

Pastor Melanie Turner-Kirkland, affectionately known as "Pastor Mel," is a dynamic preacher who preaches the word of God with conviction and power. **In accordance with Isaiah 61, the Spirit of the Lord is upon Pastor Mel and the Lord has anointed her to proclaim good news to the poor...** Pastor Mel, once a self-proclaimed atheist, had her first encounter with God in 1999. **Much like the Apostle Paul it was then that she saw God work and answered His call to salvation.** The Lord did a quick work in Pastor Mel and she immediately began to serve Him with fervor and zeal.

Pastor Mel was called to preach His gospel and was ordained a minister in June of 2004, ordained an Elder in October 2013, and began to serve as the Assistant Pastor at Mt. Olive Kingdom Builders Worship Center. In June 2014 Pastor Mel launched MK Ministries, a ministry designed to encourage, edify, empower and equip both men and women for faith-filled, prosperous, and victorious living. It is Pastor Mel's desire to change the lives of men and women everywhere she travels through the power of the Word of God.

Pastor Mel is also a proud wife and mother.

Address:	**K Ministries, Inc.** PO Box 260811,Mattapan, MA 02126
Tel:	(617) 302-7746
Website:	mkministries.us
Email:	Mkministries7@gmail.com
Facebook:	Melanie.Turner.96

FROM BARREN TO BLESSED

By Melanie Turner-Kirkland

Behold, children are a heritage and gift from the Lord, The fruit of the womb a reward.

Psalm 127:3

As a little girl my dream was to be a powerful attorney, live in a high rise, drive a Mercedes Benz, and have a daughter. I only wanted one girl to spoil and give everything that I didn't have growing up. I don't know why my dreams didn't include a husband. Maybe it was as a result of being born and raised in a household with a single mother who never placed a husband in my dreams, but I was totally fine with that. Apparently, this was my dream but that wasn't God's dream for me. Proverbs 19:21 says **"Many are the plans in a person's heart, but it is the Lord's purpose that prevails."** God had a purpose for me that was greater than my limited dream. Jeremiah 29:11 says, **"For I know the plans I have for you, declares the Lord, plans to prosper you and not to harm you, plans to give you hope and a future."** I had to learn to trust the word of God because nowhere in my dreams did I vision a husband, but that's exactly what I got, and I honestly wouldn't change it for the world!

When my husband and I married in 1997, we both had daughters from previous relationships and I made it clear that I didn't want any more children and my husband was fine with that. After giving birth to my daughter, I discovered that I was not the biggest fan of kids. I believe that some people have it and some don't; I didn't. So my husband was clear on my stance with children or so I thought. Five years into our marriage my husband started talking about

13

wanting to have a baby and of course I dismissed him. But he continued to press the issue and even got both of our daughters on board with the idea. So now it wasn't just my husband talking about wanting a baby, now he had both of our daughters in my ear constantly talking about how great it would be to have another child. Meanwhile, I was thinking, "Have another baby, who me? Not!" But their persistence paid off. After months of pressure to have a baby, they finally sold me on the idea. My daughter was now 10, and there I was, wanting to have another baby.

After the birth of my daughter, my menstruation cycle became abnormal. I would only menstruate once or twice a year and to be honest that was just fine with me. I was in my late 20s at the time, so I thought that there was no way I could be going through menopause, only to find out later that there is such a thing as early menopause. I didn't pay much attention to it when I was younger and I didn't really think that it was something with which to be concerned. I actually thought it was something to celebrate. But this "no cycle thing" became a big problem when I wanted to conceive again later in life. Due to the fact I wasn't menstruating, I also wasn't ovulating, which would make conception impossible. This problem that I ignored for so many years I now had to pay attention to in order to figure out what is going on and how we could correct it. Because now I WANTED A BABY! I started thinking about how awesome it would be to have a mix of a little of me and a little of him. I had a little of me and someone else and he had a little of him and someone else, but now we were married and I started to believe that it would be great to have a little of us running around the house.

My OB/GYN doctor was familiar with my situation as she had been my doctor for years. So when I went to her and explained that I wanted to have a child she was just as shocked as I was because she knew my stance on having more children. She suggested that I would be a good candidate for fertility treatments. I took her advice and begin treatment with a local fertility clinic in my area. Here I am, a young woman in my mid 20s and I was healthy, but I still found myself having a problem conceiving a baby with my husband. As a woman of faith I took this matter to the Lord in prayer and fasting. And as a woman of wisdom I knew that I had to exercise my faith and put works behind my faith. James 2:17 says, **"In the same way, faith by itself, if it is not accompanied by action, is dead."** So I had to couple action with my faith.

For years I was seen at the fertility clinic to no avail which only caused me to become frustrated and discouraged. Yes, as a woman of faith I became discouraged in the process. Time was passing by and there was no baby in my womb, and all around me women were conceiving and giving birth. Even young unmarried women who didn't want their babies, which if I can be honest, was making me upset! People would tell me its ok and that we could adopt, but I was adamant, I did not want to adopt! Again, I wanted a little of me and a little of him running around the house, a little person that had both of our traits and looked like the both of us. So adoption was not an option! The medicine the fertility clinic put me on regulated my menstrual cycle and I started ovulating again. With this new development in my process I was encouraged and excited and I just knew it wouldn't be long now before we conceived. We were doing everything we were supposed to do.

There were times in this process when my cycle would be late and I would get excited and run to the store and buy a pregnancy test thinking "this is it" only to be let down by negative results. This went on for two years before I got angry and told God" I'm getting off this roller coaster" because that's exactly what this process felt like, a roller coaster ride with all the ups and downs. With me thinking I was pregnant and only to be let down when I found out I wasn't. I got tired of the endless doctor's appointments and the medicine that made me sick only to end up every month with no baby in the end.

So, after years of being disappointed and emotionally depleted, I made up my mind that I was done. I called my sister one night and told her, "I'm done, I'm getting off this medicine and I'm putting it totally in God's hands!" The next day I went to church and one of the ministers came to me with a piece of paper and said God had me up all night about you. God spoke to her and told her to tell me to get off the medicine, and I was blown away because I had just told my sister the same thing the night before. She also said that God told her that I would conceive and that it would be a healthy delivery and a healthy baby, no miscarriages. I was excited about this word; it brought me hope in what seemed like a hopeless situation. I believed God! But years went by after that word and still no baby! My prayers began to shift to "God, if it's your will." Doubt was creeping into my heart and it was being revealed in my speech. Luke 6:45 says, **"Out of the abundance of the heart the mouth speaks."** I discovered that I had to be careful about what I said out loud during the waiting process. I knew that like it says in Proverbs 18:21 **"The tongue has the power of life and death."**

As time passed, one morning at church that same minister whispered in my ear God said "stop saying if." I was done; I almost fell out right there at church, because no one knew my prayer, not even my husband. But God used this woman again to encourage my heart and strengthen my faith. But again more time had passed, and still no baby! By this time everyone in the church knew we wanted a baby. Different people were coming up to me to encourage me and telling me that God is going to do it. While I knew that they meant well and God may have even sent them, it was not encouraging at all. It was only a reminder of what I longed for so deeply. I prayed in frustration and asked God "don't send another person to tell me anything about a baby until there is one in my womb!" And God graciously answered my prayer. Months went by and no one spoke to me about a baby.

One night while sitting in bible study listening to the teacher, the Holy Spirit began to speak about women in the bible who were barren and how God opened their womb and they conceived. I didn't think anything of it. Months later we were at a revival and again the Holy Spirit began to speak to me about barrenness and again I didn't think it was anything so I disregarded it. A few more months went by and by this time my cycle was regulated. But because I had been irregular more than regular, when I missed a month of my cycle it was no big deal to me. One day while sitting at my desk at work the Holy Spirit spoke to me and told me to go get a pregnancy test and I said "No", I'm not getting back on this roller coaster" and I went on about my day as normal. The following month still no cycle, but I still didn't think I was pregnant, because I didn't want to get excited only to be disappointed again. I had conditioned myself in this process not to get excited about a missed cycle. So one day yet again, I was at work sitting at my desk and the Holy Spirit said to me, "You need to purchase a pregnancy test and you need to switch those pills you are taking for high blood pressure because those ones are dangerous for pregnant women." Again, I told the Holy Spirit I'm not doing this, I'm not getting back on this ride. But this time the Holy Spirit wouldn't let me go. He continued to impress upon me that I needed to buy a pregnancy test. I said "I'm not wasting $20 on a pregnancy test." This discussion lasted all the way home. I was getting ready to turn left onto my street and Walgreens was the next left after my street and the Holy Spirit kept impressing upon me to go buy the pregnancy test. Just as I was about to turn on my street I said "Fine, you win, I'll go get the test."

I proceeded to Walgreens to purchase the test. I go home thinking this test is going to be just like every other test I have taken in the past. I put a pot of grease on the stove to fry chicken and while the grease was heating up I took the test. The test reads positive! Oh my goodness! I can't believe this, am I reading this test right? After all these years of trying and after all those negative pregnancy tests could this be real? The second line was faint so I called my mother and told her and she said "Get over here right now!" I turn the grease off and throw the pregnancy test in my bag and head over to my mother's. I'm so excited that I get lost on my way and can't remember how to get to my mother's house, which was funny because this is a trip that I took daily. I get to my mother's house and she confirms that there is a second line and I am pregnant! I call my husband and tell him, "Babe, don't get excited yet but I think I'm pregnant. I don't want to tell the girls until we confirm it with the doctor."

After hanging up with my husband, I throw the test in my bag and go pick my girls up from school. My husband and I agreed we would not tell them until we confirm it with the doctor. As I'm driving home with my girls my daughter looks in my bag, pulls out the pregnancy test, holds it up in the air, shows my other daughter, and yells out "What is this?" So now I have no choice but to tell them. I tell the girls I think I'm pregnant but I don't want you to get excited because I need to confirm it with the doctor. Everyone's excited. We try not to get too excited, but we can't help it. The next morning I go to the hospital and they confirm that yes, I am pregnant. I was 12 ½ weeks pregnant. When the Holy Spirit was speaking to me at work to go get a pregnancy test I was pregnant. The first thing the doctor said to me was, "We have to switch your blood pressure medicine."

I thought to myself, "I'm pregnant!" My promise was finally manifesting, and true to his nature the enemy kept taunting me with thoughts of a miscarriage. The first few weeks of my known pregnancy I was fearful of miscarrying because I knew so many women who conceived and miscarried. The Holy Spirit reminded me of the word the minister at the church gave me years ago and said go take the note out and read it, because I kept the note she gave me tucked away in my night stand. After reading the note, which said healthy delivery, healthy baby, no miscarriages, the fear was gone.

Today my baby is 9 ½ years old. Her name is Zoey Elizabeth. I wanted her name to represent who she is. Zoey means life because where I was barren and they said there was no life God gave me life and Elizabeth means consecrated to God. She is our gift from God so I dedicated her back to God.

My promise may have been delayed, but it certainly was not denied! Be encouraged in your waiting process. You may be delayed but you are not denied!

ABOUT

Kristina Eaton, CLC

Kristina Eaton is an Internationally Certified Life Coach who has studied alongside professionals from Australia and India; a motivational speaker and advocate for literacy. She has a passion to help, heal, restore, encourage, and inspire women worldwide from all walks of life. Kristina's drive fueled her vision and purpose into a coaching practice called Formation Coaching Group, LLC, where she serves as CEO and President. Kristina is an original and innovative writer. Kristina was honored in 2001 as a member of the International Society of Poets, for her published work. Kristina also holds membership with the International Association of Professional Life Coaches. She proudly served 15 years in the U.S. Army. She is a Bennett College graduate who studied English Literature and Psychology.

Twitter:	TheKristinaE
Instagram:	thekristinae
Facebook:	TheKristinaE
LinkedIn:	Kristina-Jackson-CLC

A CATERPILLAR LOST, A BUTTERFLY DISCOVERED

By Kristina Eaton, CLC

Like every other woman, I wanted it more than anything; marriage that is. I was addicted to the "idea" of the perfect union; it was my idol. Until one day I found myself seven months into a new marriage, living in a new city with no family, sad and alone with no affection from my husband. His attention had left the house never to return.

It all started one day when I found myself sitting in my room surfing the internet doing what I do best, looking for a husband. I had several dating profiles in rotation, especially on eHarmony. When it was all said and done, I still didn't meet anyone special. I craved a husband so bad I could taste it. When I wasn't surfing and searching, I spent tons of my down time calling this suave brother named Carlos who said all the right things but turned out to be a fraud. He came to visit me in my hometown of St. Louis and even met my family. Like a fool I introduced him as my fiancé. But when he announced that his credit cards were "tied up" I was left paying for HIS trip to come see ME. I realize now that I was chasing the fantasy of a having a man. Nothing more nothing less, "just" a man. But this guy Carlos didn't promise me anything but a false sense of security for my future. He left me empty, lost, and confused. Tapping into the love of God wasn't enough for me, I craved more. And I ended up with more than I could ever imagine.

Understand that I am a college educated woman and an Iraq war veteran and when I found myself redeployed back to the states I ended up living back in my parents' house sharing a bed with my sister, a middle schooler. I had no job, no man, and a car with no A/C. At 25, this was not a good look for me. I had been on my own for seven years and this felt like a complete setback. My savings from the deployment was running out quickly. And with my family's hands constantly reaching in my pocket, it wasn't long before all the money was gone. I was only allowed 90 days before I had to go back to my monthly battle assemblies with the Reserve. In the meantime, I was desperate and had to do the unthinkable, which was to collect unemployment benefits. But even with all of this struggle going on, I was still boy crazy.

Then along came Robert, a childhood friend. I tried to form a relationship with him because my parents thought he'd be a great match for me. But Robert and I were in different phases in our lives; I was open to settling down and focusing on having a career, while he was enjoying college life as a Kappa man. Not to mention that he declared that he couldn't do long distance relationships; trust issues I assume on his part. So I spent the next few months job hunting online, surfing the internet for a beau, and driving hours at a time to attend veteran job fairs.

One fateful day, my unemployed and outspoken self, drove my mother to work in her air-conditioned car. I've been in her office building before but never bothered to stop by the café. Because it's was 40-minute drive back to our apartment I decided to get something to eat at the café in her building. I ordered my food in and the line cook behind the counter tried to catch my attention. I finally acknowledged his efforts and returned his gestures. He told me that his name was Dan. He said that I was cute and asked me for my phone number. I thought to myself, "Well at least he's a prospect with a job."

Things appeared to move quickly after this day. While desperately looking for a job, the idea of marriage actually took a backseat. While training in Northern Louisiana, I met a colleague who assisted me with that. After several conversations and upon his recommendation, I contacted his POC, Mrs. Massengale via phone. I mentioned who referred me to her company. Then I emailed her an application. She told me there were eight available positions in various locations within 30 minutes of submitting the application. But when I called back with a decision regarding my location choice, she had gone home for the weekend. However, I was still overjoyed and filled with excitement the entire weekend thinking about how much closer I was to full-time employment. So much so, I could barely focus on training, let alone sleep.

Monday came and I called Mrs. Massengale around 9:00 am. I told her my decision about which position and location I wanted. After some coordinating questions regarding the moving process, she asked if I could be there in three weeks. My response following was, "Give me 30 days and I'll be there." The phone call ended and I had a new career, just like that! My life changed so much in that moment. I was moving from my hometown of St. Louis to Baton Rouge, Louisiana. A payday was on the horizon along with full medical benefits. I was moving out of my parents' house and things were looking up and life was good, or so I thought.

In August 2007, Baton Rouge became my new hometown. And two weeks later I found myself with a leave-in boyfriend. Yes. Dan moved in with me after being terminated from his job. I felt ashamed of my new status because I believed that it was beneath me to cohabitate. So I demanded that Dan marry me. And four months into my relationship I found myself engaged to a complete stranger. I went from damsel in distress to live-in fiancé. But this was what I craved so badly, to find a man that was willing to marry me. The devil delivered exactly what I had ordered, but it cost me. At the time I just didn't know to what extent.

I knew absolutely nothing about Dan besides his name, hometown, age, and his SS#. Well, maybe a little more. But Google seemed to know more about my soon-to-be husband than I did. Nevertheless, despite these facts, in December 2007, exactly eight months after Dan and I met we were married. I somehow believed that marriage would cure my spiritual convictions; so I eloped without any family present for the ceremony. Dan's friend Tyrone stood in as a witness for my husband. On that day, anxiety filled my entire body and I perspired badly all day. I had no peace in my heart about what I had done. So one day, my mother kept asking, "Are you sure you want to do this?" Little did she know that it was too late for me; the deed was done. I was a Mrs. And when I look back at the pictures taken on my wedding day, the discontent and regret on my face was painfully obvious. Months passed and we traveled as a duo and fought like it was World War III. Not knowing who I married didn't help either. My plan was to make him into what I wanted him to be. I know I had a lot of nerve. I was trying to do God's job.

Things went from bad to worse after marriage. Dan always needed to have control over everything. I was more than uneasy. My life as a newlywed was full of anxiety. I was stressed out and completely naïve about what was going on around me. My nights were loveless and empty (literally) even though I prided myself on being a perfect wife. At night home-cooked meals were a given (except weekends). I was doing what I thought I was supposed to do. It was just the two of us, and we were supposed to conquer the world as best friends. But that didn't happen.

Tyrone became the third wheel of my marriage, without my knowledge or consent. If walls could talk in my house, they'd tell all about Tyrone and my husband engaging in all types of things like smoking marijuana on our patio while I wasn't home, attending the local clubs together, and arguing as if they were a couple. Let's not mention the video-game-playing love affair that would keep my husband away from our home, even if I was sick. When I confronted my husband about his behavior with Tyrone he didn't seem to care. One day I declared that Tyrone was no longer welcome in MY house and he just laughed.

Loyalty had found another address and I fought to regain my position as the queen of my domain. But you can't regain a throne that you were never truly given in the first place. My love languages were not only disregarded, but they were never learned. When I purchased our first home, Tyrone came around more. My husband stopped asking me to go out and I wondered, "What had happened?" All the signs were there, but I just didn't see them until a one mildly cool day with a gentle breeze. I remember walking outside the back door onto the driveway where Dan was standing. I approached him, then leaned in to kiss him. As soon as our lips touched he jumped back as if he had been stuck with a long needle. He looked me in the eye and said, "Stop, don't do that!" I was floored, shocked, and devastated. I was no longer wanted; the desire was gone; the attraction nonexistent.

I continued to take lots of mental notes at this point based on my husband's distant behavior and lack of attention. The state of our marriage was poor. Saturdays were my days for unwinding at home from the stressful work week. One Saturday afternoon in particular, Dan left his cell phone by mistake and after hearing it constantly ringing, I decided to answer it. And lo and behold, it was Tyrone. He had been calling all day. I was livid. But I calmly told him that "Dan is at work, he left his phone and I'll have him call you back once he gets off. You don't have to keep calling every hour on the hour, just leave one message." Of course, he got an attitude. His response spoke volumes. Once I picked Dan up that night from work and told what had occurred he just laughed as if it was normal. His response spoke volumes without him speaking or mumbling a word. The red flags were waving; the light bulbs were flashing. At that point, our marriage was officially done. I couldn't compete with a man and I wasn't going to.

I was afraid to dissolve my union based on the guilt and shame that is the stigma surrounding divorce in the Christian community. However, I couldn't see myself with this man over the next 10 years and I didn't want to bring any children into the marriage under such circumstances. Besides, I wasn't going to let him take my dream of motherhood away from me. In all honesty, I knew that I could do better and I that's exactly what I did.

A sorority sister of mine recommended an attorney, S. Lee. I didn't really know much about her, so I Googled her and searched the Yellow Pages. I found nothing, but because I was so desperate to begin the filing process, I hired her against my better judgment. In January 2009, I paid Ms. Lee a $1,500 retainer fee and filed for divorce. There was no joint property nor were any children produced from the marriage. The divorce should have been cut and dried. But six months later I received a call from Ms. Lee requesting more money to finalize my divorce. I wondered what she had done with the money that I had already paid her. After some research, I discovered exactly what paperwork it took to file for divorce and the timeline in which to do it. It turns out that Ms. Lee was a family law attorney and divorce wasn't her specialty. I told her that I had hired another attorney (I found him in the Yellow Pages). Mr. Fitzpatrick was great at only a fraction of the cost and his work took less time. Ms. Lee had the nerve to ask me, "Is he white or black?" I replied "That's not important, he's doing the job that I paid him to do." She then says, "Well, what is he charging you?" At this point Ms. Lee and her inquiries were stepping on my last nerve. I ended the call saying, "I think we've discussed everything, goodbye."

By December of that year I found myself a 27-year-old divorcee. It was one of the most pivotal and challenging years in my life. Grieving my marriage was significantly more difficult than fighting in combat. I felt every emotion imaginable: anger, sadness, abandonment, rejection, devastation, and the worse of them all, depression. I was angry because my husband didn't want me and there was nothing I could do about it. I was sad because I was alone and didn't know my identity outside of being Dan's wife. I went into my cocoon that no one knew about it, nor had access to it. One of the most embarrassing times was going to church every Sunday and the usher asking about my husband's whereabouts. I said he is working; eventually I stopped going all together. Despite the time that I knew him before getting married, the man that I loved and committed my life to had rejected me and then abandoned me. My spirit was crushed. The devastation of my failed marriage overtook my thoughts. I thought I was a failure and believed that no one was ever going to want to marry a divorced woman. I asked myself, "Will God ever forgive me?"

For weeks I walked around the house feeling numb, not wanting to eat and crying uncontrollably in the silent darkness. No one could really relate to what I was going through so I suffered alone. The energy of the house felt very cold and the house post- divorce was suddenly very big and empty. Lying in the bed, not being able to sleep, I couldn't even talk to God. And I didn't want to. I didn't know what to say, I had no words. Peeling myself off the bed day in and day out to prepare for work was an absurd chore to say the least. I was numb spiritually, but my body continued to go through the motions. At work no one knew my pain. I would close my office door to cry when I felt the tears coming. My game face was believable and convincing even though I literally wanted to die. My brokenness and vulnerability caused me to enter into a tumultuous relationship prematurely before I had totally grieved my marriage and completely healed. I started going to a divorce support group at a local church. With every meeting I was getting better and purging out all my emotions. The devil thought he had me, but God said otherwise. I was in transition from being Dan's wife to a journey of self-discovery. Six years later, after my "aha" moment, I made a drastic change in my spiritual walk. I fasted with my home church, worshipped in my bathroom, and prayed in my closet. I read my Word like never before, faithfully. One afternoon after Sunday worship service, I broke down crying and couldn't stop. I just kept saying" It's so hard, it's so hard." I was living for God wholeheartedly in the purest and saw no rewards for my obedience. It was hard to give Him total control; I would question God. "Lord, where is my husband? Where is he? I'm not getting any younger." I completely surrendered to God; He had my full attention. My long suffering and sacrifice were well worth it.

In October 2015, I met my current husband. We met at a jazz event at my friend's church. I was invited about 10 days prior via text message. The text said, "Jazz Event Saturday, bring a date." I had little to no interest about the latter part of this text. I had two possible men that I could invite, asking either of them to accompany me was a waste of time in my opinion. However, I tried, and neither was available. I didn't want to go for many reasons. Two hours before the event started I notified my friend that I was not coming. She insisted that I come anyway against my frame of mind. I arrived late and food was being served. Plate in tow, I spotted my friend and her husband and sat with them. The one chair left at the table was next to my current husband. That night I found out that he was God-fearing, attentive, a good listener, and so much more. God had revealed to me that my husband would be short and have five letters in his last name. I was obsessed over this known fact. That night when I met my husband, he turned out to be 92% of what I asked for in my life-changing prayer.

Some of my priceless treasures that I possess today are the peace of God, blessed finances, an air-conditioned car, total self-confidence, self-identify in Christ, and home ownership, just to name a few. Like many women, I was always trying to do things my own way on my own terms, but I discovered that when I did it God's way and had the patience to endure my prayers for the perfect husband were delayed but they were not denied.

ABOUT

Detrick Harper

Detrick Harper is a Certified Life Coach, Motivational Speaker, and Women's Empowerment Coach. He is also the owner of U Matter Life Coaching Services and member of Dimensioned Wellness Life Coach Network, the first of its kind. As a proud graduate of The Life Coaching Institute of America, Detrick has a passion for inspiring and empowering women and teen girls by motivating and inspiring them to unlock and live their best life. He assists in educating them on empowerment by teaching the concept of loving yourself first. His motto is *"If you don't love yourself how in the world are you gonna love somebody else?"* He aims to see everyone, not just women and girls, but all people, discover the power of self-love and to find and fulfill their God-given purpose in life. Born and raised in Texas, Detrick currently lives in the great city of Houston which is home to the Houston Texans.

Facebook	umatterlifecoaching
Periscope	Detrick Harper@dillan1981
Instagram	umatterlifecoach
Website	www.umatterlifecoaching.com

WHO AM I???

By Detrick Harper

Life! We all are born into a world by a woman, whether she is married, single, dating, scared, lost, or alone. The blessing God bestows upon her to carry and deliver a living and breathing person into this world can never be compared to anything else imaginable.

I was born in 1981 to a proud mother and father who thought they were finished having kids. The youngest of three children I have always been different from the beginning. I was destined to survive after being born on the bathroom floor of my grandparents' home with my umbilical cord wrapped around my neck.

As early as I can remember I always felt different. I remember all the way back to the first grade sitting in class looking and listening to all the other kids and how they were interacting with one another. Boys playing rough, spitting, and getting dirty! While girls were playing with dolls, twirling their hair, and talking about Barbie dolls. I didn't know what it was about me that caused me to feel like an outcast. I just knew that what I was seeing and hearing around me totally was not how I saw myself. This was the first time I can remember asking myself the question and not really knowing the answer but "WHO AM I?"

As a child you're told by your parents, peers, and society how as a male or female you should behave in this society. Growing up, I wasn't the kid who was "liked," so I spent a lot of time with my grandfather. When I look back now, he gave me what I know now to be unconditional love. Every day I came home from school excited as I got off the bus to run home to be with him. I was bullied, teased, and called names at school by the other kids all day long and never told anyone, but somehow this guy could always tell when something was wrong with me. We discussed everything, and he always knew how to take my mind off my childhood troubles.

It is said, "All good things come to an end," and on May 3, 1991, after a regular day of school, I got off the bus and ran home to the one person that I knew truly understood me. I expected to see his warm, welcoming smile. Instead I walked in to my grandfather lying in the middle of the floor gasping for air; trying to holding on for dear life. Being only ten years old, I didn't know what to do, so I ran to him and held him in my arms, weeping, watching as my tears of mourning dripped on his face. God took my grandfather to where we hope to all go one day, Heaven!

From that day forward my life began to spiral out of control. I fell into a deep depression. Not only had I experienced rejection from my peers at school, but now I felt abandoned. He left me and all I would do is cry alone in a dark room sheltering myself from the world. I grieved for years without sharing with anyone the hurt and pain I was feeling and going through. I told everyone I was alright. It was the first time I learned how to lie. I was afraid of showing or telling anyone how I truly felt. I was afraid that one day they too would be taken away from me.

Life moved on and I entered junior high school. I laid low and did not allow anyone around me to get close to me. My parents loved me and showed it as much as any parent could but I still didn't feel loved and found it hard to adjust to life.

Once I reached high school things got worse, due to the bullying I was getting day in and day out. At 15, I tried to commit suicide by cutting my wrist. A year later I took a bottle of pills and this time I came face to face with death. After this I vowed to myself that I would try my best to understand why God kept me alive on this earth. The question of "WHO AM I?" came up again.

Despite all the turmoil that was going on, I was a kid that loved to smile, dance, and have fun. Even though I was bullied for many different reasons, I still had a passion to love, nurture, and help others. After high school, I finally felt like I was getting around to being me. I was constantly finding myself in situations where people were clinging to me saying they loved my high spirit and were intrigued by my welcoming demeanor. As good as this felt I still couldn't see my purpose. So, I started dabbling with drugs and alcohol to cope with the reality of not wanting to deal with or face who I was. I did drugs for about 15 years straight and was totally addicted without anyone ever knowing.

In spite of my inner struggle, I still managed to empower and inspire people with my words of encouragement and undying passion to help others. What I didn't know was that God was not through with me yet! Another tragedy happened that was the breaking point in my life. A very dear friend was murdered. This was a reality check for me. The spirit of God moved so fast in my life until before I knew it, I didn't have any desire to do drugs, drink, or go to clubs. I realized that life was too short and I needed to find myself and stop wondering "WHO AM I?"

I thought my purpose was helping others in the healthcare industry. I joined an awesome church that I loved. While these things helped, I discovered that just waking up and going to work was not enough. After years of this, I stepped out on faith and quit my job. I asked God to completely come into my mind, body, and soul and lead me to my purpose. I hit rock bottom literally! No money, no job, no car, and rent was past due, almost in eviction status.

A friend I worked with at a previous job knew about my quest for purpose, called me one day and suggested I become a Life Coach! I heard of this profession before, but knew very little about it. I responded "Life Coaches are people who coach and teach people to set and reach attainable goals in their life and help make their dreams come true by living their best lives, and that's not me!" Her response to me was "Whether you know it or not, the whole time we worked together you did just that for me. You completely changed me, my husband, and my kids' lives with the advice, direction, and encouragement you gave. You told me that I can do anything I wanted to do, as long as I put God first and believe I can do whatever I put my mind to."

Without even knowing it I had been coaching her, all the while giving her the tools she needed to fulfill her dreams and start accomplishing the goals she set out for herself. This was the first time I actually felt what I was doing came natural to me and that I could be stepping into my purpose. I wondered if this could be my calling. Because of the huge change I made in her life, she felt a need to return the favor by offering to pay the full tuition for me to become a Certified Life Coach. She believed in me that much! Once I received my certification blessing after blessing started coming from everywhere. I joined a life coaching network. This network was started by a woman who overcame her own trials and triumphed. After learning about this network, the rest was history. My life has not been the same since. Not only has my life changed but I no longer have to ask "WHO AM I??"

I am a man of God who loves to empower and inspire people using my life struggles, trials, heartaches, and pain to encourage, teach, and motivate others to feel and know they can have anything their heart desires. I am a man who also knows his purpose and knows why he's here and understands his TEST was leading him to have a powerful TESTIMONY! I am also a the proud business owner of U MATTER LIFE COACHING, where I specialize in one-on-one coaching, motivational speaking, and empowering people to live their best and happiest lives!

So if you ask "WHO AM I???" I'll simply tell you that I was just someone who was "DELAYED but not DENIED."

ABOUT
Ericka S. Johnson, M.S.

Ericka S. Johnson-White, M.S., is a Life/Empowerment Coach, Human Services Professional, Certified Fatherless Daughter Advocate, Motivational Speaker, Facilitator, and Mentor. She is certified in domestic violence advocacy, addictions counseling, sexual assault, divorce and family mediation, and victim-offender balanced restorative justice mediation. She is the Founder and Creator of Empowered 2B Invincible Coaching, LLC. She is a member of the Greater Atlanta Section National Council of Negro Women and a member of The Black Life Coaches Network. Ericka is a graduate of Rust College in Holly Springs, Mississippi, where she received a Bachelor of Social Work degree. She received her Master of Science in Criminal/Social Justice from Lewis University in Romeoville, Illinois, and a Master of Arts in Human Services at Concordia University Chicago.

Presently, she is a student of Coach Diversity Institute pursuing life coaching certification under the mentorship of Dr. Towanna B. Freeman. Ericka continues to give back to her community by helping women and young girls that are destined for greatness by being laser focused in uplifting, motivating, educating, and empowering in her purpose-filled vision. She is helping others uncover their God-given gifts and live out their purpose to overcome the setbacks and receive victory in the very things that have broken them. Ericka was born and raised in Chicago, Illinois, and now resides in Atlanta, Georgia. She has one daughter, Brooklynn Skylar McCall.

Website:	www.lifecoachericka.com
Email:	info@lifecoachericka.com
Facebook:	empowered2Binvincible
Twitter:	lifecoachericka
Periscope:	LifeCoachEricka
Pinterest:	LifeCoachEricka
Instagram:	lifecoachericka
LinkedIn:	Ericka Johnson, M.S.

BRUISED BUT NOT BROKEN

by Ericka S. Johnson, M.S.

I was born on May 21, 1973. My mother was only 18 years of age and my father was 23 years old at the time. I grew up on the Southside of Chicago in the Auburn Gresham section. During the school week I lived with my grandmother on 69th Green in the Englewood section of Chicago and on the weekends I stayed with my mother on 8824 S. Lowe. When I was in the 5th grade I moved to live with my mother full time and attended Ryder Elementary School. And that's where my childhood journey began, in a neighborhood full of gangs, violence, and drugs. However, it was also a family-oriented neighborhood where everyone knew each other. Both of my parents grew up on that same block. When I was two years old, I climbed out of my baby bed to find my father, Aaron White, laid out in the bathroom tub; he had overdosed on heroin and morphine. My memory has been permanently stained with the vision of the ambulance arriving and the stretcher passing me, being pulled by paramedics with the police escorting them.

The majority of my life I've been a fatherless daughter. Truth be told I've also been for the most part a motherless daughter if I include the absence of a real mother-daughter relationship. The absence of my father and my estranged relationship with my mother has never gone unnoticed by me. I never really knew if it was that my mother never really knew me or if it was the twin brothers of an old boyfriend of hers who tried to molest me in our own home that made me so bitter. Thanks to my strong tomboyish ways back then, which allowed me to fight them off, they never did succeed and only got away with some forced kisses.

I often used to ask God why I didn't have a good relationship with my mother like everyone else. But I never sat still long enough to hear a response. So I just kept moving on with my life as I knew it. I was an only child so my support system was my childhood friends. I always dreamed and desired a family without the dysfunction and I chased love most of my life. I would keep myself around crowds of people to always feel needed and secure.

Because of my exposure to living in a home of continuous domestic violence, alcohol and drugs, I vowed that would never be me. But those very things I said wouldn't be me ended up being me. I always said my drugs of choice were alcohol and love. I also had a passion for contemporary dance and so did my best friend, Chanda Ross. We were very good at dancing. It was our outlet but we never continued due to the lack of support and guidance we needed. The Chicago Public School System was never that great, so to expect an honor student out of me, coming from the environment I was in, was a setup for failure. I went to an average elementary school and high school. I never had anyone encouraging me to get good grades and to be a scholar. I never felt the need to impress anyone, including myself.

Throughout my teenage years I had several boy crushes and always thought I was in love. But what really was love supposed to feel like? I didn't have any real male figures of influence in my life, so I really had no idea what a real man looked like. People always said that when you finally love someone you will truly know it. However, when I did think that I had found love, that saying turned out to be true. I really did know it. He was not only my first love, but he was my drug. He was my first EVERYTHING, even though I secretly had an abortion without his knowledge. It was years later before I was able to bring myself to tell him. It took a lot of work and time for me to get over that journey. He's actually still one of my best friends today. Those were the good times. Then it was back to reality, living in the grown up world after college. My life was just beginning, or so I thought.

I was living the life. I was working a government job. I had my own car, my own place, and nice money in the bank. Yet somehow I still felt lost. I always knew I was supposed to be doing something much greater. I asked myself daily, "what is it that I'm missing?" I used to cry myself to sleep at night, feeling lonely and fighting depression. I found myself smiling and laughing amongst friends and coworkers, knowing I was empty inside. I started thinking maybe I needed another degree, and that would make me happy and more complete, right? I completed a Master's degree program, which made me the first of my family to graduate from college and receive a Master's degree.

Even after all of this something kept tugging at me at night. I worked ten years with the State of Illinois working as a Caseworker, conducting interviews and determining eligibility for food stamps and Medicaid. There was always a bitterness in me and I got tired of seeing others happy and living their life.

The life I thought that I was supposed to be living. You see, I thought being complete was to be married before you were 35 years old. I also thought life was supposed to include love. I chased, struggled, sacrificed, begged, pleaded, and accepted anything, just for love. A close friend and I, someone whom I consider to be a mentor of mine, Kimberly Tennial, is to whom I would go when I needed advice and when I had my moments of confusion. She told me one day "Ericka, you have to love yourself before you can love someone else." I never knew what that really meant at that time. That's how lost I was, for real, I didn't know what that meant. Love myself? I don't even know who I am!

So I continued to go through trials and tribulations going from one relationship to another. I was holding grudges for years with people who had no idea I was even mad. Sometimes I didn't even know why I was so bitter and mad. I felt somebody owed me something for the attention and guidance on which I missed out. There were years of walking around just lost because I had all the luxuries of a good life but was still so unhappy.

Then I started dating an old high school sweetheart whom I had reconnected with online. He was familiar to me. And as we got to know each other it seemed as if we both we wanted the same things in life. We fell fast in love and the next thing I know, I quit my so-called good government job, withdrew down my pension, and moved to Dallas, Texas, where he was living at the time. This was the first time in my life I felt whole, secure, and happy, or so I thought. I was not really sure if I was making the right choice at the time. But I told myself that it was impossible for me to mess up any more then I already had. So this was the start of a new journey.

Things were awkward from the start. My partner owned a house, but for some reason when I moved to Texas to be with him, we lived in an apartment. But I overlooked that because he had some crazy reason that made sense at the time. Most of my time there was spent planning for our wedding. But the next thing I knew, I was pregnant and diagnosed with gestational diabetes. Then, out of nowhere, the person whom I thought I knew was not that person anymore. He changed. And it was dramatic. I suspected that there were other women. All the signs were there, but I had chosen to ignore them. My grandmother used to always say "When a man really likes another women, he will get mean and you best to get out of his way, because you're in his way now."

I had my baby girl via C-section. I was happy, but the very next day my man began to fight me. Never in my life have I ever heard of a man fighting a helpless woman. This was the beginning of the end. I had a newborn baby and everything went downhill fast for me and this man.

By the time I had my baby all of my money had run out. We got evicted from our apartment because this man wasn't paying the rent. I lost everything from my car, clothes, shoes, and furniture. Most importantly, I lost myself, my mind, power, spirit, confidence, and self-worth. It wasn't until I found myself surrounded by the most filthy dirty beige walls of a cockroach-infested place called the Shangri-la Motel on 3712 W. Davis Street Dallas, TX, for two weeks, did I have my epiphany. It came in the midst of the confusion in my head and the second heartbeat under my breast of my sleeping newborn baby. As I carried my newborn baby with me in my jacket to the corner store it all became clear. I was finally away from that dirty place this man had brought me and my newborn baby to live. That night I had only five dollars to my name, but I knew that God was preparing me for the process of the rebirth of me.

I told my partner that I needed to go back to Chicago that night. He agreed. So he purchased a ticket and dropped me off at the train station. He kissed me and the baby goodbye and said, "See you soon." I thought I was on my way until I reached the ticket counter and discovered that he had given me a fake ticket. Thank God for a Good Samaritan behind the ticket counter because she allowed me and my baby, who I was holding in my arms, on the Amtrak train.

Thankfully, I made it back to Chicago with one bag and a little baby. I communicated with maybe only five friends. I isolated myself from any and everyone else that I felt didn't have my best interests in mind. I stayed with my mother for about a year. I had no job, car, hope, faith, or self-worth. I was mentally lost. I gained weight, had stress disorder, and was postpartum. I was diagnosed with depression and diagnosed with diabetes yet again. I found myself back on insulin and pills again. I was a zombie just walking around with no purpose.

The only thing that stopped me from suicide was the grace of God. Because only the lord knew how many times I had suicidal thoughts. All I did was pop pills and sleep; I couldn't even properly give attention to my baby due to depression and postpartum.

I had to quit the first job I started after a few months because I had uncontrollable crying at work and could not concentrate. I had been isolated so long I wasn't used to being around people anymore. I developed a hot temper, and I would get angry and defensive when I felt a person was disrespectful or just being mean or bossy. I would have outbursts and irate behavior with everyone. A coworker of mine at the time, and a dear friend to me today, Natasha Dowdell, was the very first person who even recognized my brokenness. She spent her own personal time with me and we had very intense talks. I started going to sleep with the Christian channel on. After my long talks with Natasha I started opening up to other close friends who were the only sources that spoke into my life on regular bases. I started reading about my conditions and decided I didn't want to be a victim anymore, because I wasn't really mad at the current situation. I was angry with myself and it's hard to forgive yourself.

I tried going back into the environment in which I felt more comfortable, and that was the classroom. I had become obsessed with learning and I thrive in that arena. I enrolled in graduate program at Concordia University, and that's where I met Dr. Kisha E. Hart. My enrollment in her course was the beginning of my healing. She helped me more than she realized because she didn't know what I had just been through. I know it was God directing me in the right direction, not to get another degree but to start placing distinctive people in my life. I finally started to realize what reason, season, and lifetime really meant. Dr. Hart affirmed me and made me ask myself real questions about my purpose and being an agent of change. In a blink of an eye I started a journey of self-awareness, which was something I'd never explored for myself.

I got reinstated with my good old government job and worked there another two years, bought a car, and moved out of my mother's house to my own place with my daughter. I went back to church and started going to seminars, conferences, and workshops and reading self-help books. I attended anything that dealt with self-help or personal development. I started to feel again. I stopped crying, built my confidence back up, and took back my power. I realized what was really making me unhappy, and it was because I didn't know who I was. I had no purpose nor was I operating in my God-given gift. That tugging in the middle of the night was God directing my path. I had to get somewhere quiet and listen for his response. I had to change my mindset and change my circle of friends and replace the old people with great people around me.

I was going to work knowing something was still missing. So I kept asking myself "What's wrong now?!" I got quiet and waited. I'm not supposed to be here, not at this job. There are greater things waiting for me. I stepped out on faith and quit my good old government job. I was determined to have enough courage to discover my gift and walk in my purpose. I always knew I was destined for greatness, I just didn't know how and what that greatness was. Once it was revealed to me, everything I was always seeking came together. I was supposed to be exactly where God wanted me to be. I endured everything I went through to bring me to where I am today. I declared to be the best mother that I can be. I declared victory over the very things and people who tried to break me. I declared to walk and operate in my purpose with authority and elevate other women in doing the same.

You see, all along I've always tried to fix situations myself. But I had to learn to be still, call on God and what God has for me is for me. What I learned from life coach and mentor Linal Harris is that you can't just walk around without knowing your God -given gifts and purpose for your life. Knowing your purpose, power, and possibilities is inevitable to really make it in this world and to be truly happy and fulfilled.

You see, I thought being married and having a family would make me whole because society, friends, and family seem to say so. But I know now when I'm walking in my purpose and believing what God has for me will be for me, then all other things will come into in alignment with my life. I discovered that I had to find out who I was first, but I had skipped that step. It wasn't until years of hurt, disappointment, struggle, and several adversities did I realize that I didn't know why I was on this earth. I thought I was seeking love but realized I am love. God gave me someone to love me back unconditionally and my beautiful baby girl became my love. Everything I lost could be replaced. Today I hold my own power and I know that I am enough. I love myself. I am resilient. So you see I was never broken, just bruised.

"Throughout my journey the most profound lesson I learned was to free yourself, you have to tell your truth, but most importantly you have to tell it to yourself."

Life Coach Ericka

ABOUT

Audrey L. Woodley

Audrey Woodley- a woman of power, charisma and influence - uses her platform to speak, teach, and coach women around the world.

Serving as a Motivational Speaker, Life Coach, and Brand Therapist Audrey applies principles from her own life as a native of Chicago, Illinois, a single mother, a successful entrepreneur, and co-author of two International bestselling books to help women entrepreneurs reach success. Faith, she often tells her life coaching clients, is one of the most valuable tools and building blocks of any woman's success when applied persistently and consistently.

Audrey is best known as the Brand Therapist, helping women identify solutions to brand challenges. She uses new-age problem-solving tactics, proven social media strategies, effective marketing communication, and customized brand identity coaching. Audrey's own brand has seen great success, including features in several magazines that focus on women entrepreneurial ventures. Additionally, Audrey has been invited to speak at various functions including several workshops presented by Senator Kimberly Lightford. Audrey was a guest speaker at the highly acclaimed GHGF Prayer Breakfast, a Life Coach speaker for "Make-Up & Martinis" event, and keynote speaker for Changing Oasis, Inc. events.

When it comes to speaking, coaching, and consulting women entrepreneurs Audrey Woodley delivers!

Webiste:	www.audreywoodley.com
Facebook:	AlwoodleyCEO
Twitter:	LWoodleyCEO
LinkedIn:	Audrey Woodley
Instagram:	audreywoodley

HOW C.P.R. REJUVENATED MY LIFE

By Audrey L. Woodley

At one point in my life I was a wreck. So many unsolved situations had piled up on top of me and had broken me into many pieces because I didn't know my worth, and I did not know my faults. Because I didn't know these things, I kept repeating the same cycle. The truth is that some situations were beyond my control, like the fact that my Mom was terminally ill with less than six months to live and I didn't know what I was going to do. Also, my bank account was dead (no money) and some of my entrepreneurial ventures were draining the life out of me. As far as I was concerned, I was surrounded by death. The underlying condition of all of these situations was fear, which left me feeling paralyzed, afraid, and alone. So, I began to pray this prayer: *"God, I want abundance for my life, and I accept the repercussions of my actions, but Lord, I need you now. I need you to take my hand and give me your direction. I've tried to do it by myself over and over, my plate is empty. I've run into so many brick walls and I'm broken. I know I deserve better. Remind me whose I am so that I can rely on who and what I am."*

I needed to step out on faith and be the Audrey Woodley I was born and purposed to be. I knew that faith without work was dead, so I jumped into action. I relied on my Vision, I corrected some of my faults, and I connected with like-minded women and I began to walk into my purpose. God turned my mess into success. Becoming a published author was one of my top goals for 2013 and a part of my life's vision. At first, I had no idea how I was going to accomplish this goal. Then through my varied networking activities, I connected with an opportunity to become one of 30 nationally well-known professional business women who would go on to co-author an anthology book called "Network to Increase Your Net Worth," which was compiled by Toni Coleman Brown. My plan was to make an affordable but worthwhile investment in my dreams that would provide good financial return and opportunities to expand my business and brand. I worked my plan and the plan worked but not without my hard work. I created a marketable platform that allowed me to increase the sales of a book that I co-authored (part of my vision) and I toured Chicagoland speaking to and networking with groups of other successful entrepreneurs and women. My brand gained more visibility and credibility. These are all goals that I planned and wanted to achieve. By doing my due diligence, I was able to identify a real opportunity for the growth of my personal brand.

God was bringing me back to life. He gave me CPR. My dead situations were resuscitated and brought back to life. When most people think of CPR, the first thing that comes to mind is that someone is hurt, unable to breath, experiencing helplessness, possibly in need of mouth-to-mouth resuscitation, or in need of a defibrillator to bring them back to life. But I received a different kind of CPR. God gave me the kind of CPR that heals broken lives. He gave this to me in my time of need so that I could live and breathe again. I was revived and invigorated with the strength and the direction needed to see my true value.

I have always been smart about was turning to God in times of trouble or confusion and asking Him for help. I recognized that many of the situations that I consistently found myself in were similar in nature. I was like "God, I'm tired of repeating the same mistakes over and over again. It seems like I'm going around circles never making real steps toward progress. I need you to show me how to solve my problems the right way," and that is when He gave me The 7 Principles of C.P.R. and they are as follows:

1. Know your worth - Psalm 40:1-2
2. Know your vision - Jeremiah 29:11
3. Know your faults - Philippians 2:3-4
4. Forgive yourself - Genesis 33:4
5. Plan your goals - John 16:13
6. Live your dreams - Hebrews 11:1
7. Walk into your purpose – Luke 10:39-42

My definition of CPR is Condition, Prayer, and Reflection. I've discovered that for every problematic challenge/situation there will be a condition you have to pray about, reflect on, and release.

Sometimes life's challenges can hit you so darn hard that you think you're in a nightmare but the pain in those challenges lets you know for a fact that you're not dreaming and that those challenges are real. This is where The 7 Principles of C.P.R. come into play and can be utilized to help anyone in solving their problems.

For example, if you've been in several relationships where you have gotten the short end of the stick, the Principle KNOW YOUR WORTH could be helpful. If you don't know who, what, and whose you are then you won't settle for anything that life throws your way. By settling for what people think you should get in life, you will take disrespect, lack of recognition, and less of everything that you're fully entitled to.

I know that many times I get caught in habitual ruts because I tend to go back to the same excuses. These excuses that keep me from succeeding haunt me. Excuses like," I don't have enough money to invest in my own business." "I don't know how to develop my own program." But I make a liar out of myself every time I take money and purchase things that I don't need and that won't give me any return on investment.

Then there is condition that involves a lack of planning. If anyone ever find themselves not prepared for a program or a business, they should simply Begin to Plan! This is when I encourage you to apply Principles II and III. KNOW YOUR VISION or what do you want out of life? And, KNOW YOUR FAULTS, or what is it that is really holding you back? Is it fear? And, if it is fear, of what are you afraid? Do you look at other people's successes, including some of your friends' successes, and say to yourself, "I wanted to start the same type of business but my friend has started hers and now she's doing her own thing." So what? If it was a good idea before she started her business, it is still a good idea. Don't be afraid of the challenge to start your business and don't make excuses. Accept the challenge and prepare for what God has in store for you.

Then pray and ask God to help you remember the strengths that you possess that can help you solve your problems as well as recognize and avoid those faults that hinder your success. Prayer is your connection to the Holy Spirit, our comforter and guide. Be willing to change for your own benefit. We all face challenges, issues, or problems but we should all understand that we don't have to face them alone.

God is waiting to help us as soon as we ask Him for help. Reflect on the scripture that the Holy Spirit gives you, it is part of your roadmap to success and will assist you with your plan to excel in life. God gives us million-dollar ideas and daily downloads, and we can only begin to manifest them if we are not constantly distracted by our problems. You can also reflect by journaling. Write down the lessons God shows you, and see how living in today's uncertain times can be used to push you forward. Finally, when you reflect on the past challenge(s), you will see that change (changing your mindset and changing bad habits) was necessary in order for you to succeed.

I am so grateful to God for giving me these CPR Principles. I am proud to be able to share them with the world. In my life I've had quite a few hardships and setbacks, but life is funny. You make plans and God laughs. However, I will never stop moving forward because my true success may have been a little delayed, but it has never been, nor will it ever be, denied. I'm taking my newly resuscitated C.P.R.'d life all the way to the bank.

ABOUT
Maryam Smith

Maryam Smith is President/Founder of The Keys to Unlock Your Silence Inc., a non-profit organization that is committed to helping victims of domestic and sexual abuse go from being victims to becoming victorious. Being a survivor of domestic violence and an overcomer of sexual abuse enabled her to do something that she spent years not knowing how to do, and that was unlocking her silence. She realized that her true healing would only come from her speaking up and about the abuse that she'd encountered. Her unlocked voice wouldn't only serve purpose for her healing, but also bring healing to the many other individuals that are too afraid and ashamed of unlocking their voice because of the abuse.

She is now embarking on a long-time dream of becoming an author. At the age of 35, Maryam successfully completed a long-term goal obtaining her bachelor's degree in Social work. Being a single mom for the past 19 years inspired her to not to only do better for herself, but to be better for her daughter.

Tel:	347-336-6579
Email:	unlockursilence@gmail.com
	jbonkers97@yahoo.com
Facebook:	Maryam Smith
Twitter:	@unlockursilence
Instagram:	unlockursilence

ALLOWING MY PAST TO PASS

By Maryam Smith

"Listen, you can't say a word to anyone because if you do you will get in trouble. So I am going to give you this change and you will go buy yourself some junk food and keep your mouth closed. Remember, if you say something it's you that's going to be in big trouble, not me."

How many children have heard this and are still keeping their mouths closed? This was me for most of my life. I kept my mouth shut to the point that it made me experience a sickness from which I was fortunately able to recover. The unfortunate thing is that many people never recover from the stains of sexual abuse.

My birth was a result of the actions of two immature teenagers. The world I was born into was one that often had me wondering how so many individuals managed to survive. This world was super unfair in my sight, and had no respect because many things were allowed and are still being allowed to be swept under the rug. This is especially true with sexual abuse in African American families.

When I was barely settled into grade school, I was robbed of my voice and was too young to even understand what I had or even how to get that voice back. It was tough for me. Over time I've learned that if there was nothing else that I would cherish it would have to be my voice. I have learned that not only is it necessary, but it is also a very powerful tool.

Having to face the sexual abuse head on isn't something anyone, no matter your age or sex, is ready to deal with, yet way too often a child is exposed and scarred for life from this indecent exposure. Within my culture, folks are quick to chastise a sexually abused young girl, who may be acting out her abuse by running around loose in the neighborhood, by telling her to stop being a fast behind and by telling her that she should keep her tail in the house. But what the family should do is seek answers to make sense of that young girl's behavior.

I made so many mistakes and bad choices in my adolescence all the way up to my late twenties because of my abuse. It formed and shaped my life before anything else had a chance. I learned at an early age how it was so much easier to just lock away my silence. What I didn't learn at an early age was that my body was a temple. That I belonged to the Most High God in the heavens who would love me unconditionally despite the mess I was making out of my life! I also learned at an early age how it felt to be misunderstood because of the lack of communication that took place between me and both of my parents. It was at an early age that I also learned how to be prideful, realizing that somewhere throughout the process I had been stripped of my humility and it was quickly replaced with pride. I picked up this arrogant attitude to try and hide the pain, anger, and frustration that I was really carrying. I learned that my body possessed power over the minds of young boys and that I controlled when and how I dealt with them. I learned aggressive behavior because of all the garbage I had kept stored away inside.

The sexual abuse did something terrible to my self-esteem. Not having a father to play an active role in my life didn't help. So, by the time I was sixteen I was involved with an older guy who spoiled me as a father would his daughter. I loved the attention that I was getting so much so that I didn't realize how little we had in common. The void that I thought he was filling was only getting deeper and deeper. Looking for love in all the wrong places was a true statement for me. Especially when I didn't know the right way I was supposed to be loved. I myself didn't know how to love someone the right way either. In that relationship I would go on to experience domestic violence firsthand. At first I thought the behavior to be a bit of a turn on. I, like so many others, believed that behavior of such violence was actually how some expressed they loved and cared for you! Boy, was I confused and had to learn the absolute hard way! I later on learned that being sexually abused would only open the door for you to be domestically abused especially if you haven't received the adequate help that is needed for one who has been through sexual abuse.

I spent so much time wondering "Why me?" Why did I have to go through such horrible things? I didn't receive an answer to those questions until my thirties. I mean, on top of all the abuse I still had to go through bad treatment. In particular from certain close family members that I thought would always have my back. The hate they displayed for reasons of which I am totally unaware was terrible. It got to the point where if we were to see each other on the street there would be no effort made for communication to be exchanged. Sometimes I couldn't even give a glance.

One day while driving in my car a gospel song came on and started to minster to my soul. That song had given me the answer to the question that I'd ask myself over and over again! "Why Me?" But this time, the usual answer of why NOT me, came into my spirit. I discovered that my voice wasn't just for me, but it was for millions of others to hear and understand. At that point I was given the Keys to Unlock My Silence. And I knew that I could take those same keys and give them to someone else to unlock their silence. I cried and cried because I couldn't believe that God would use this broken vessel to help the healing process of other broken vessels. This was a task that I deemed too great for me to partake in, so after following the voice of God I knew that my greater purpose was using my voice by speaking out against the abuse.

Almost right away, I knew that The Keys to Unlock Your Silence needed to be carried and birthed through me. There were three keys that I used to help me through my healing process: my voice, my confidence, and my faith.

The first key is my voice. I had to learn that my voice needed to be heard about this matter because so many manage to keep theirs locked away for most, if not all, of their life. My voice was the key to not only unlocking something in me, but my voice would be the master key to help others who feel that something inside of them needed to be unlocked.

The second key my confidence. In order for me to be able to use my voice I needed to rebuild my confidence level which was at an all-time low. In order for my confidence to have been built to the level I needed it in order to grow I had to come to terms that none of this was my fault. Once I understood that I wasn't the cause, I noticed that I grew stronger and stronger in my confidence.

The third and last key my faith. I had to learn that without it I wouldn't have been able to start this mission or accomplish anything. I had to understand that my faith wasn't in me believing in myself as much as it was me having faith in God. It took me a long time, but I had finally begun to understand why I had to go through the things that I had gone through. I didn't know how this was going to come to pass but what I did know was that this was God's plan for my life. I knew that if I would just walk towards all that I know he has for me then endless doors of opportunity would begin to fling open.

Being a risk taker by nature converted me into a faith leaper and because I leaped out on faith I am now the Founder and President of The Keys to Unlock Your Silence, a non-profit organization that was Incorporated in October of 2014 and recognized as a 501c3 entity in February of 2016. I know that this is not only the beginning of my journey, but the start of millions of souls being saved by the Keys I have to offer. What I have learned throughout the years is that it is not always about the impact you make on those you know as much as it is on those you don't know. Confidence in God has helped me to understand that my voice will always have a place in society and to never, ever lock away the sounds of healing. So now, instead of deeming myself as damaged goods I deem myself as refurbished goods. Strong enough to withstand a makeover and be able to shine like brand new all over again!

It is truly amazing to see just how far I've come by the grace that has been on my life! I never knew the importance of unlocking my silence until I got over myself and understood I was created for greater things.

Every day I wake up not only to inspire but to also be inspired. I never thought that success would feel so great. I achieved success just by unlocking my silence. So now, when I'm asked to define success I simply define it like this:

"Success is not how much money I've accrued in my life nor is it determined by the position or title that I may hold, but success to me is having been through so many trials and tribulations and throughout it all coming out victoriously."

ABOUT

Dana Rose

Dana Rose is the CEO and founder of DDR Consultants, founded in 2009. She has extensive years of experience in the real estate mortgage and foreclosure process. DDR Consultants is a multi-service center that provides a variety of services to the residents of Westchester, Putnam, Dutchess, Nassau counties, and New York City. The services include: Foreclosure Document Preparation, free consultation for summons & complaints, qualified written requests (QWR), and Property Management Solutions. Dana Rose is also a content provider for The Total Faith Network which is a lifestyle, Entertainment and Info/News Christian program of experienced innovative technology that airs worldwide. She is the host of "Women's Voices by Dana."

Her background in public relations has prepared her to be the Co-Pastor and Vice-President of Upon this Rock Ministries, Inc. in Mt. Vernon, NY, a ministry that was created to help develop a strong community to be able to deal with the challenges of crime, drugs, poverty, illiteracy, and inadequate housing by the spiritual demonstration of compassion for the purposes to assist in eradicating urban community problems. She is the Senior Outreach Coordinator of the Family Restoration Project of the Lower Hudson Valley, a wraparound collaborative initiative to help support the successful and safe transition of young fathers from detention, out-of-home placement, or incarceration to their families and communities. She collaborates with key partners in the Lower Hudson Valley Sub-Region to give a thorough, composed project for lessening recidivism and advancing public safety.

Email: danadavis914@gmail.com
Facebook: dana.rose.9693
Instagram: danadavis914

THE OTHER SIDE OF THIS

By Dana Rose

In order to fully understand how God uses adverse situations to bring us to a place of peace, I've learned to be still. I've also learned through the trials and tribulations of life that HE is all I've ever needed. In fact, HE is all I've ever really had. Sometimes in life, circumstances may bring about interruptions. Many years ago I received the biggest interruption ever. My mother was diagnosed with stage III cancer and given eight months to live. At that very moment, my faith journey began and it was tested and tried in every area of my life. After numerous sessions of chemotherapy, radiation, and prayer, my mother, Thelma Lee Hunt- Davis, was called home to be with the Lord in August of 1994. This was hard for me to fathom. But what was even worse is what happened next. Within precisely five months after my mother's death, my brother was murdered. He was an innocent bystander whose life was cut short in his prime. He was also an inspiring hip-hop artist who had received notice the day before that he was being signed to a deal with Sony records. He was my inspiration and the "big brother" that anyone would have wanted to have. After this tragedy, I thought the worst was over, but then I received a call from the VA hospital exactly two days after the death of my brother with someone stating, "I know that your family is going through a very difficult time, however I have to bring you bad news that your father, who was stable just this morning has suddenly passed away." "My God!" I screamed. At that point I knew that God's hands had to be on me. Because how could one individual have the capacity to remain steadfast amidst these traumatic events and still manage to display strength, stability, and faith, while seeking a career at the same time.

It was hard for me to believe that in just five months I had lost three immediate family members that I cherished so dearly. I realized there had to be something on the "The Other Side of THIS." Sometimes it would seem as if the broken pieces in my life were never going to be put back together again. But I learned that as long as I kept on developing my faith in the living God that I could still rise. Sure, it took time for me to shake myself loose, but I had to look over all of what I was going through in order to be resolved and to allow God to heal, restore, and fix it. I had to get out of my own way and allow God to take control, not only so that I could be prepared in the off chance that there were any future trials.

I said "future trials" because I discovered that my trials were not yet over. In July 1999, my 16-year-old stepson was unjustly shot and killed. He was a star football player in high school at the time. This new tragedy devastated our family, especially my husband and my other two sons. Trust me when I say that it was only because of my experience with being steadfast in my prior circumstances that allowed me to hold it all together. I leaned on my faith and just knew that there had to be something on the "The Other Side of THIS." Before, my husband was there to comfort me, yet now, even in the midst of my agony, I had to comfort and console my husband. I also had to learn with my sons' grief that "mothering" had to quickly rise to an altogether different level because of this catastrophe. I often wondered, how can one even speak when tragedy hits you by surprise and makes you speechless? It was only because of my faith that I was able to survive.

After many years of healing, my husband and I decided to purchase a house for our family. "The Other Side of THIS," was starting to manifest itself in my life. Surprisingly, we got the house with limited finances and an unfavorable credit score. My husband said that he had heard from God and that all we needed to do in order to get our hands on the property was to claim it and it would be ours. Within seven months we closed on a beautiful four-bedroom house with a five-car driveway. This house became the place where we all began to rebuild our lives and reestablish our goals. My husband began to build his own accounting business called Esor Accounting Services that proved to be very rewarding. His company would assist non-profit organizations throughout New York City with their financial reporting. Our family was working together in faith to build our ministry as well as our business, all while keeping God in the forefront of our endeavors. Because we were faithful to God, we received His favor and started ministering together at the County jail on weekends. We saw that we needed to offer back to others what had been given so freely to us. Before long, my husband and I became pastors of Upon this Rock Ministries, Incorporated. Our vision was and still is to see the salvation of those who have been lost due to the hopeless conditions of our inner city neighborhoods. Our mission is to see their minds renewed by the power of God, not only by assisting them in their spiritual growth but also by interacting with our community in a way to remediate the social and educational challenges that plague the neighborhoods we have been called to serve. Working in the inner-city where economical, educational, and health issues are in large numbers became our obsession.

We very quickly became a resource center for the underprivileged. People began to flock toward our calling. After several years of growing a successful ministry and rising to community prominence, we experienced a major political, religious, and legal setback as scandal and false allegations came against my husband. The residual effect of this scandal caused our family to lose a large portion of our six-figure annual income. My husband was wrongly convicted and subsequently imprisoned for two years. However, God has always provided for us. And my husband, being a servant of God and highly educated, was able to write his own appeal to the Supreme Court and was released early by decision. He also became the first inmate of the facility to pastor to the entire inmate population. It was then that I knew that there definitely was something on "The Other Side of THIS!"

The many challenges in my life helped me to discover who I was and just when I thought they were over, more showed up. One morning around 10:00am, I received documents from the bank regarding my home. The one thing I did not need at that moment was a lawsuit. It wasn't a lawsuit, this time, but due to the loss of income, my home had gone into foreclosure. Right then and there my feelings were so feeble. Because my husband was not present at the time, I didn't know where I would go. I began to pray. Being a prayer warrior, I have always sought the Lord first. The Lord began to speak to me and announced that I would survive this battle despite it feeling as if I was under an insurmountable opposition. I kept my faith! As I looked into the Summons and Complaint against me I started to ask the Lord, "What should I do?" Having a background in business was not what I needed at that moment. What I needed was a lawyer. God began to reassure me that everything would turn out fine. It was so risky yet at the same time

I moved within a surety that God was my advocate as I was reminded of a scripture, Isaiah 10:27, **"And it shall come to pass in that day, that his burden shall be taken away from off thy shoulder, and his yoke from off thy neck, and the yoke shall be destroyed because of the anointing."** A promise of God may be delayed but his word tells us it is not denied.

I was reminded of yet another Biblical account regarding the prophet Daniel and the delay he experienced in the manifestation of his request to God. Daniel 10:1-12 says that Daniel was a man of boldness. He was not hesitant to ask and trust God notwithstanding when it was unlawful for him to do as such. When I was faced with foreclosure, I felt a sense of shame. I also felt as if I was a failure. I was worried about the negative effect that this would have on my FICO score. I knew that these types of things could impact any future real estate purchases and even my ability to rent an apartment. Like many people, being faced with foreclosure, I felt helpless. In any case, I still believed that there was something special waiting for me on "The Other Side of This!"

Once I understood the foreclosure process, I discovered that there were practical strategies that anyone could utilize to save their home. God gave me, through His favor, an individual who helped me, and a crash course in the foreclosure process in order to gain the knowledge and direction I needed. Again my faith was activated! And little did I know that a business was in the making. As I began to share and educate others about challenging the banks about ownership of their property and how important it was to respond to any complaint within 20 to 30 days, DDR Consultants came into being. DDR Consultants is now a multi-service center which provides a variety of services to residents in Westchester, Putnam, and Nassau counties as well as the five boroughs of New York City. DDR Consultants was birthed out of my own personal experience. We focus on getting the best possible results for those in need. Our mission is to educate those who want to learn more about the foreclosure process, which has become an epidemic in our nation. We also provide assistance to families facing foreclosure by helping them to find alternatives through research and documentation. There are so many homeowners who have been affected by predatory and abusive subprime mortgage lending practices. While DDR specialists are not lawyers, we make sure that families know their rights and we guide them to the appropriate legal counsel in New York State. DDR Consultants has become my "Other Side of THIS." We have been blessed with a 100%

success rate for our clients. We keep folks in their homes! I am often so pleased with the smiles I see on our clients' faces because of the work that we have performed.

My past has made my present more powerful! Not only has the birth of our business placed me on "The Other Side of THIS," but the same has been true for Upon this Rock Ministries, Inc, a faith-based 501(c)(3) organization. Within this company we created a program called the Family Restoration Project of the Lower Hudson Valley Sub-Region (Westchester, Putnam, and Rockland Counties). It is a collaborative initiative to help support the successful and safe transition of young fathers from detention facilities, out-of-home placement, or incarceration back into their communities and with their families. With other key partners, we are working to lessen recidivism and advancing public safety, and enhancing results for young fathers returning home from incarceration and veterans returning from tour of service.

I've learned that we should never let our circumstances cause us to lose hope. While trials and tribulations are often beyond our control, our behavior and how we respond to these trials mean everything. During my trials, I never lost sight of my dreams and aspirations. I didn't allow my situation or people to break me. My victory might have been delayed, but it wasn't denied. Under the weight of intense adversity, I learned to understand that what we call PAIN, God has called it PREPARATION, as when you have faith and hold on, you can get to "The Other Side of THIS!"

ABOUT

Crystal K. Melton

Although raised in suburban New York, Crystal K. Melton considers herself to be a southern girl at heart. Born in Clinton, NC, her parents relocated to Harlem USA before her first birthday. However, her love for the south developed over the years while spending her summer vacations in North Carolina with her family. It was during these times that her strong faith in God and love of family would be reinforced.

Crystal spent her formative years in Queens, NY and was considered a book worm, as she would rather read then play jump rope. She continued her education at Cornell University where she studied Consumer Economics and Housing. With a strong desire to help people, her career would lead her to work in various positions where she taught and trained at some of the top 100 financial firms in the United States. Her career would also allow her to travel extensively and experience many other cultures.

Crystal's vision is to inspire thousands of individuals to live their best lives. She has been blessed to speak before groups of women all across the country from the boardroom to the pulpit. In July 2007, she became an ordained Elder and serves alongside her husband at Christian Light Missionary Baptist Church in Long Beach, NY. Crystal resides in Freeport, Long Island with her husband of 26 years, Bishop Designate Isaac R. Melton, Jr and their daughter, Loren.

Website:	www.getfreecoffeenow.com
Facebook:	CrystalMelton
Facebook Fan Page:	Inspire923
Instagram:	ogmelton
Email:	cmdestiny2@aol.com

I CAN SEE CLEARLY NOW

by Crystal K. Melton

As I lay in my bed with the covers completely covering my head I began to ask a question many of us at some point in our lives have asked, "Lord, why me?" On that particular day I didn't hear the reply, so day after day I asked the same exact question, determined to get an answer. I believed if I could just get an answer it would help me to understand why I was in the situation I found myself in and then maybe, just maybe, I could pull myself out of this deep depression and state of despair. I was so desperate for answers or just one answer, that for weeks on end I asked the same question so many times that it became a routine. "Lord, why me?"

As my husband would prepare to leave for work, I would sit on the side of the bed. Each day I would kiss him goodbye and tell him to have a great day with a big smile on my face. I couldn't let him know what I was feeling inside, it was just too much for me to even try to explain or put into words. As I look back I realize he probably knew. Once he was out the door I would listen for the car to pull out of the driveway and then I would climb back into my bed, which became my place of refuge, cover my head with the comforter and ask the same question over and over again." Lord, why me?"

Sometimes I would continue my monologue by trying to explain to God why it shouldn't be me. I'd plead my case by confessing how I tried to love everyone or how I wasn't a bad person. I tried to explain to God how much I loved him and then I would ask God, "Why are you punishing me? What did I do wrong?" This routine became my new normal. And as time passed people actually began to treat me as if everything was normal, but deep down inside it wasn't. I was hanging on by a thread and a very thin one at that. I'm sure by this time you are probably wondering what in the world could have possibly happened to me to bring me to the brink of a mental breakdown.

Well before April of 2001, life was good. Really good. I had been married for 11 years to my childhood sweetheart. He was the love of my life and my best friend. I was his ride or die chick. Together we were building a wonderful life. We were working together in ministry at our church. We had just purchased our first home and were driving two very nice cars. Family was good. We were blessed beyond measure. My career was amazing. I had a job that I loved teaching technology, time management, and organizational skills at some of the world's top firms. My job afforded me the opportunity to travel all over the world flying first class, staying at four and five-star hotels. I felt like I was on top of the world. The Ivy League education was truly paying off and literally I had surpassed my goal of earning a six-figure income and being a leader in my field. Again, life was good. I shopped whenever and wherever I felt like it. We ate at the best restaurants and money wasn't an issue because I knew the next paycheck or bonus was right around the corner. You might as well say we were living the American dream.

Little did I know my life was about to take a major detour. I will never forget that dreadful day. It was Resurrection Sunday morning. The sun had not yet even risen but in our faith it is our custom to celebrate the resurrection of Jesus Christ all day and to specifically come together for sunrise worship at 6am. I awoke with anticipation of the glorious time that we would have all day in worship and the delicious Easter dinner that was already prepared for our family. I was even more excited as I was assigned to bring the sunrise message for the first time at our church. It was only a few months earlier that I had answered my call to the ministry. So, as you can imagine, I was super excited. So much so that I actually woke up earlier than need be, you see I was not a morning person and found myself on most occasions running behind schedule, much to the chagrin of my Pastor and husband. The normal custom in our marriage was that whoever wakes up first leans over gives the other a peck on the cheek and say good morning. A little cheesy right? I know, but it was a great way to start every day.

On this particular morning, as I opened my eyes and leaned over to kiss my husband, I quickly realized that something was horribly wrong. For some reason I could not see his face, I could see the outline but it was like someone had taken an eraser and erased his forehead, eyes, nose, cheeks, and mouth. Nothing was there. At first I ignored it, maybe I needed to just wash my eyes and it would be ok. So after our morning greeting I went into the bathroom and looked into the mirror, and to my disbelief I could not see my own reflection, and now I was beginning to feel anxious. I grabbed my washcloth off the towel bar, ran some warm water, and began to bathe my eyes. I closed my eyes tightly, lowered my head, and began to pray, "God, in the name of Jesus let me see when I open my eyes." I waited a moment then lifted my head, opened my eyes, and looked toward the mirror. To my disappointment there was still no change. I simply could not see.

At this point, I was no longer just anxious. I was now scared as a sickening feeling landed in the pit of my stomach. The tears started to flow from my eyes as I returned to our bedroom to tell my husband that I couldn't see. It felt like the words were caught in my throat. I didn't want to even say them and I absolutely did not want to hear those words out loud. What had happened in the span of nine hours, from the moment I laid down to sleep to the moment I had risen, was horrifying. My vision was almost totally gone. My husband has a very calm demeanor and this particular day was no different. If he was concerned or scared, he was really good at hiding it from me. He took me by the hand and we returned to the bathroom to attempt to wash my eyes once more. I don't remember how many times we repeated this process and prayed to no avail. Through tear-filled eyes my husband tried to console me and tell me it would be alright. Yet I wondered if it really would be. "I can't see," is what I continued to cry out. So he helped me get dressed to go to church.

We got in the car for the drive from Long Island to Queens, which is usually a short 20- minute trip, but on this day it seemed as if it took us forever to arrive. I remember it just like it was yesterday as the tears continued to fall on my pristine white suit. He took my hand and held it tightly as he continued to steer the car with his other hand. My mind was racing. I thought and wondered what was I going to do? I needed to see, I had to see, there was just no other option. In less than thirty minutes I would stand before our congregation to bring the Easter morning message. How would I read my notes? As we pulled up to the church I kept waiting for that calmness I needed and wanted so badly to come over me. But it never came; at least not that morning.

My husband came up with the idea to magnify my notes on the computer so that I could see them. It was a great idea but it did not work. I know that it is only God's grace that got me through that day and the days and months to come. I was told that the message I preached that morning was powerful. I give all the credit to God because I don't remember what I said or much of what transpired on that Sunday morning. Matter of fact, the rest of that day was all literally a big blur.

The next morning I woke up hoping and praying that my vision would be restored. It's funny, I remember wanting to hurry up and go to sleep so I could wake up in the morning and this nightmare would be over. Well, to my disappointment when I woke up, my vision was exactly the same. No better, no worse. We immediately began the journey of trying to figure out what was going on with my vision. We made appointment after appointment to see specialist after specialist. I began to feel like the woman in the bible with the issue of blood. After going to doctor after doctor I was no better and even grew worse, maybe not physically, but definitely mentally. My mental state was worsening. It just seemed like no one could figure out what was wrong with me.

One long arduous day after being examined by several doctors, the last doctor asked me if I would stay a little longer. He wanted his friend, a specialist in the field, to take a look at my eyes. He believed if anyone would know what was wrong he would. At this point, what did I have to lose? The doctor entered the room, and I could sense that he expected to see a much older woman after reviewing my chart. I remember him being very warm, attentive, and caring. He had a calmness about him. Thank goodness, because I was probably a little grumpy at this point. He examined me and within a few minutes he looked at me and said, "I believe I know what is wrong, I need to just run a couple of tests." I was cautiously optimistic. None of the previous doctors even had a clue. After the results of the test returned he was sure he knew that I had a rare retina disease. I began to cry out of joy and relief. Finally someone had a clue. But my joy was short lived as he gently informed me there was no cure for my rare disease. I couldn't believe what my ears were hearing, with all the technology that existed in the world, what did he mean there is no cure? I screamed, "You have to be able to do something!" Desperation was in my voice. My hopes began to flee and that pain in my stomach that had been there for weeks came back even stronger.

We immediately began treatment that would hopefully prevent my vision from getting any worse. Emotionally I was a wreck. The huge doses of steroids I took daily certainly didn't help. Everyone around me walked on eggshells as I was ultra-sensitive. At any moment, and for no explicit reason, I would explode into a tirade or become a sobbing mess. I attended weekly doctor appointments to make sure the steroids were not causing any damage to my body, such as diabetes. The great news was that in spite of the side effects it seemed to be working. The doctor told me the inflammation from the disease was almost gone and I started seeing some improvement in my vision. They began the process of gradually weaning me off the steroids. I was told it was because it is such a powerful drug that if I just stop taking them all at once it would have detrimental effects on my body. I was just glad to be done with that part of the journey and I am sure my family and friends were as well. For my final doctor's visit I was really excited to hear the report. As he examined my eyes he told me that the good news was that all the inflammation was completely gone and that he didn't see my eyes getting any worse; however the not so good news was that scar tissue had formed, blocking my central vision which is sometimes a side effect of the steroids I had been taking. So as a result your vision will be permanently damaged.

I felt like I was having am out of body experience. "Really? You can't be serious, there has to be something that can be done," I said. I knew I needed to look on the bright side of things. At least my vision would not get any worse. And, for a moment I did feel better. Then I began to think about how I had not been able to fulfill my job responsibilities in months although I was still receiving my full pay! Reality was slowly beginning to set in that my life as I knew it was about to change drastically. After a year of prayer and soul searching it became evident that my only option would be to resign from my well-paying position and apply for permanent disability.

With some trepidation this is what I did. I hated the thought of being labeled disabled and that only added to my level of depression. While waiting to be approved on disability our bills were climbing higher and higher. We still had to pay the mortgage, insurance, and credit cards (of which I had several). My husband and I watched our savings and retirement funds dwindle pretty rapidly. After about 18 months, I was finally approved for disability and the blessing was the fact that the approval came after applying only once. So many people had told me that I would never get approved the first time. Well I did. Now the shock came when I realized my disability was literally one third of my previous earnings. We had grown accustomed to living a certain lifestyle. But in what seemed like a blink of an eye that all changed.

The blessing in all of this was the fact that in all that time our marriage grew stronger and so did our reliance on and faith in God. We never went without shelter, clothes, or food on our table. The lights may have blinked once (if you know what I mean), but we even turned that into a romantic candlelit evening. We may have needed heating oil on a couple of occasions, but that gave us the opportunity to snuggle together.

And so the day came when I heard the answer to my question, "Lord, why me?' And I heard the answer. God had answered me the first time I asked the question, but I just didn't want to hear Him. The answer was quite simple. He said, "Why not you?" I realized that this was the opportunity for me to show the world a measure of God's grace and mercy. On that day I got out of that bed and came up out of that pit of despair and depression. I washed off the ashes from my face and I truly surrendered my life and will to God. I began to express to Him true gratitude for all things, even my hard places, for it is the Apostle Paul that stated to count it all joy when he found himself in difficult situations. I have truly learned to rejoice even in challenging times for I know that God can do all things. As a result I began to see God as my provider; not a well-paying job, not my Ivy League education, but He became my true source.

And although in terms of income it was a great deal less, God began to restore as he did for Job. Instead of one home he allowed us to purchase our second home and use the first as an investment property. He began to show me my true purpose in life, what he created me for, and he sent a new career, one that I love. This new gig allows me to help, inspire, and empower others. Our ministry is flourishing and doors are opening for both my husband and me. Doors we never thought would. We are now living an abundant life. I can hardly believe it has been over 15 years since this event, but I am so grateful for my journey. I am blessed with a unique and keen spiritual sight that could only come from God and this is what I know without any doubt that by faith I am already healed and my vision is restored! I can see clearly now.

ABOUT
Cathleen Williams, Minister, RN, Esq.

Cathleen is a powerful life coach, and inspirational speaker, deeply passionate about helping women live life to the fullest. She brings to her clients and audiences the compassion and wisdom of a single mother, the tenderness of a Registered Nurse, and the keen assessment of an attorney. Cathleen is also a licensed minister and graduate of New York Theological Seminary.

Cathleen is the author of "Single Mother the New Father," an important, powerful book series for single mothers.

Find Cathleen here:

Website:	www.cathleenwilliams.com
Facebook:	cathleenwilliamsesq
Twitter:	CathleenEsq

KEEP YOUR EYE ON THE PRIZE

By Cathleen Williams, Minister, RN, Esq.

"For I know the plans I have for you," declares the LORD, "plans to prosper you and not to harm you, plans to give you hope and a future. "

Jeremiah 29:11

It was a cool fall morning. I remember slowly walking around campus without any real idea where I was going. My mind was in a fog as I pondered the news I just received from my father. He told me that Lincoln University had informed him and my mother that they needed to come and pick me up. Due to my dismal academic performance from the past two years, I would not be allowed to continue my academic studies. I was being dismissed. In translation: "Your daughter ain't gotta go home, but she's got to get the hell up outta here!"

I would not be allowed to register for any classes, I would not receive any counseling or emotional support, I had to surrender my dorm room within 24 hours, and I would not have any help from the university to store my things or move them all off campus. My time at Lincoln University was over.

My emotions spiraled between feeling embarrassed and devastated, to manipulated and abandoned, and then to plain old dumb. I was nauseous, crying, and disoriented, but I kept walking. As I passed through the crowds, students were milling around. Some were chatting and walking with friends, while others were laughing with excitement and positive expectations for the new semester. In my mind, however, everything was moving in slow motion.

As I approached a bridge, my thoughts began to drift. Looking for any way to escape the pain I was feeling, I stood on that bridge and wondered "What if I jump? I could just be done with all of this if I just jump." As I thought about that option, I began to sob uncontrollably. As I stood there, barely able to keep my balance, the saving grace was that a jump from the bridge was barely high enough to leave me with broken bones, much less a loss of life. I certainly didn't want to deal with a broken ankle or leg while trying to navigate my move off of campus.

It was hard to believe that two years earlier I was graduating with honors from the High School of Music and Art in New York City. My parents never had any trouble with me as it related to school. I loved school and it was obvious in my grades. I was an excellent student who passed all classes. I scored very well on SATs, Regents exams, and all standardized tests. In addition to being a good student, I participated in all kinds of in-school and afterschool activities. Where I really excelled, however, was in the classical orchestra. I had accomplished so much as a classically trained cellist, that I was second chair in our orchestra of very talented musicians, and was also in the All Borough Orchestra.

I was primed for college, and had a bright future ahead of me. If I graduated, I would become the first person in my immediate family to become a college graduate. Being the first in my family to graduate was not my motivation to go to college. I wanted to go because I wanted to further my education and I loved school and the academic environment. However, there was a lot of pressure on me to be successful.

While my parents were not college educated, they raised their kids with the specific directive – get a good education and go to college, no questions asked. My mother was a nursing assistant and she knew a Black female doctor who worked at Bellevue Hospital, and that became her measure of success. My parents wanted me to be a doctor, and I applied and was accepted to Howard's Pre-Med program.

The only problem was that I never wanted to be a doctor. For as long as I can remember, probably before I even knew what a lawyer was, I wanted to be an attorney. Growing up as a little girl I was fascinated with Perry Mason. I loved to watch him investigate criminals, and interrogate them until they melted on the stand. Perry never lost a case, and never even had to prove one. I wanted to be just like Perry.

Unfortunately, my parents didn't really believe that a little Black girl could become a successful lawyer. In their time it was not common to see a female lawyer, and it was even less common to see a Black female lawyer. My mother believed that for a woman to be successful in a thriving career, she had to go into medicine. My father believed my mother and she decided this without my input, and pushed me in that direction. I made the decision to abandon my dream, and adopt my mother's as my own.

Two years later, on that cool morning, I stood on the bridge, crying and staring at the ground below me. As I stood there, unable to move, I realized I didn't want to die. I just wanted to escape my pain. With every ounce of courage in my body, I walked back to the dorm, and started making arrangements to move off campus.

I used to blame my beloved mother for my failures. I thought that had she not pushed me to go into medicine I would never have flunked out of school, and I would have been a lawyer years earlier.

The reality was that my mother wanted the best for me, and she sacrificed her dreams so that I could have financial security, live a life of influence and power, and contribute to my community. She knew that life for Black women in America could be a living hell, so she wanted to position me to be successful. She acted out of unconditional love for me and I could never be upset with her for that.

My mother was a Jamaican immigrant who came to this country with nothing. She and my father overcame tremendous odds as Black immigrants in America in the 1950s, and they wanted more than anything for their children to never struggle or suffer like they did. The courage I found on my last day at Lincoln came from the lessons they taught me.

I left that little bridge on the Lincoln University campus, and I packed up my things and moved on. I found a beautiful, small apartment in the nearby town of Newark, Delaware. I went to the local Christiana Mall and found a job in a retail store, and I enrolled in continuing education classes at the University of Delaware. I took courses in political science, writing, and history. I worked hard to raise my grade point average, and when I did I was offered full-time admission to the university.

My advisor recommended that I consider a Bachelor of Science in Nursing, since the university was willing to accept all the science courses I completed at Lincoln. Pursuing this degree meant that I did not have to start over, and I graduated less than three years later.

Looking back many years later, I saw that so much of what I wanted to achieve in life was delayed, but not denied. Graduation, my primary goal, was delayed. Courage, strength, faith, and determination kept my dream alive long enough for it to be realized.

And when I graduated from the University of Delaware, mom and dad were as happy as they could be.

I ended up having a successful nursing career working at two of the most prestigious hospitals in the country. It turns out, helping people as a nurse was closely aligned with how I wanted to help people as an attorney. However, my dream of practicing law would also not be denied.

Even in my nursing career, I could not suppress my love for investigating matters. I loved questioning things and finding answers. I was a seeker of justice and always wanted to be on the right side of it. As time passed, it became clearer that I had to be a lawyer.

I started to save money, and took classes to increase my GPA enough to apply to law school. I took the Law School Admission Test, scored very high on it, and because of a lot of hard work, determination, and sacrifice, I was admitted to The Ohio State University Moritz College of Law. I graduated (on time), and passed the New York State Bar on the first try. Another dream delayed, not denied.

In the heat of the moment, standing on that bridge, contemplating jumping, I could not see the blessing before me. Years later, I know I could not have been more blessed. I didn't become a physician, but I did spend a great deal of time in medicine healing people, caring for them and their families, and advocating for their health and well-being. I truly never thought of nursing as a career, but when I found it, I found a love that has lasted many years. Not only do I love what the nursing profession stands for, but nursing provided me with the resources and inspiration to follow my dream of becoming a lawyer.

I learned from my experience that being denied can sometimes be a set up for a miracle to happen. It can really be exactly what I need. I also learned that if I keep pressing forward, that denial will likely prove to be a delayed reward that is greater than anything I could imagine. In other words, if it is something is meant for you and God ordained it for you, you will never be denied. Whether it is a relationship, a degree, a job, a career, whatever it is, if it's for you, it will come to pass. It might not happen when you want it to, but it will manifest.

After my experience at Lincoln University, there was a great deal that I needed to accomplish, personally and academically. There were many lessons I needed to learn, and I needed them to become a better student, a better woman, and a better mother. When my dreams were realized, I had more gifts than I could have ever imagined. Now, standing up for myself and others comes naturally for me. I am an advocate for the oppressed, the underrepresented, and the unrepresented. I enjoy helping people solve problems, and helping people in crises become whole again. I enjoy exposing injustices and promoting peace and equity wherever and whenever I can. After all, that is what Perry Mason would do.

ABOUT
Jamee-Marie Edwards, MPH

Queens native Jamee-Marie Edwards is a literary enthusiast and lifelong artist. Her zeal for writing was fueled at an early age by her grandfather, who would take her out to Rockaway Blvd and tell stories as they watched the planes take off and land. As an author, Jamee-Marie particularly enjoys sharing stories that will empower her readers. One of the mottos she lives by is to become inspired so you can become an inspiration.

Jamee-Marie loves the Lord and her desire to encourage others extends to the various creative arts ministries of which she is a part.

Jamee- Marie holds a Master's in Public Health with a concentration in Health Education and Promotion from Benedictine University and a B.A. in Communications from Adelphi University. In 2013, Jamee-Marie made her debut as an author with her Children's Book "But I am a Cat!" She is also the Founder of "The Me I Need To Be" Empowerment Program, which encourages participants to discover, embrace, and celebrate their unique gifts, talents, and abilities.

"It is truly a blessing to be a co-author in the Delayed But Not Denied Anthology. I am excited about this new season in my life."

Instagram:	kyshia_marie_lawrie
Facebook:	AuthorJameeMarie/
LinkedIn:	Kyshia Marie Lawrie
Periscope:	Kyshia-Marie
Twitter:	@JMarie_Edwards
Website:	www.maeinspireu.com

COURAGE TO SOAR: RELEASING MY BUTTERFLY WITHIN

By Jamee-Marie Edwards, MPH

And there he was, tall and slender, wearing a blue jacket, denim jeans, and a baseball cap, just as he described on the phone. As I slowly pulled into the restaurant parking lot, he turned around and our eyes met. Something stirred in my spirit and I knew it was him. At 45 years of age, the very man I longed to meet was standing right in front of me. Yes, there he was, my biological father.

During his visit to New York, my father and I had several opportunities to spend quality time together. These moments revealed similarities that reached beyond our undeniable resemblance. We even had a chance to experience the father/daughter carriage ride I dreamed of. However, as time passed there were some gray areas I needed to personally work through, as a result of this newly found relationship. To be more transparent, I was in need of some spiritual counseling sessions to work through my roller coaster of emotions. As the sessions progressed, it became evident that God was using this situation to do an inner work in me. Meeting my father was truly a blessing but, the deeper sense of self that emerged reawakened the butterfly within me.

You see, I was at a crossroads in my life. One that required some leaps of faith that would transition me from who I was to who I was created to be. Although, my purpose was clearly evident from years ago, I had yet to muster up the courage to fully walk in it. I dibbled here and dabbled there, leaving the true essence of myself feeling cheated, unhappy, and frustrated. And it all boiled down to how I let my fears stifle my faith.

To give you a visual, there is a picture I adore of a blindfolded woman, standing on the edge of a cliff, with the extended hand of God strategically placed beneath her footing. This leap of faith moment resonates with my spirit for two reasons. For starters, I have been on that edge several times before. But, I have to admit, there is a big difference between the woman's posture and mine. The artist would have to depict my hands maneuvering the blindfold trying to get a sneak peek as opposed to them resting at my sides. And we all know the true essence of faith does not operate like that, which brings me to my second reason. Every so often this picture flashes into my subconscious as a reminder that "God's Got Me." But even still (in capital letters), I would find myself operating in fear.

An example that vividly comes to mind occurred in my 30s. As a nurse I always appreciated the teaching aspect of the career. So, I was more than thrilled when I secured an opportunity to teach at a school that trained nursing assistants. I felt free and it was indeed a "butterfly moment," especially after being unemployed for some time. However, three weeks into the job, the unexpected happened and I found myself in a "cocoon moment," as darkness ensued all around me, literally. I became ill and began to slowly lose my eye sight. The progression of my sight slipping away felt like the aperture of a camera closing in slow motion. It was indeed an unsettling and frightening experience.

I was diagnosed with a condition called Iritis. The bout from start to finish lasted for three months. The condition was in both of my eyes and my vision became so blurred that at one point I could not decipher anything and only saw shadows. So much to the point that someone had to tell me, "your vegetables are on your plate at 3 o'clock and your meat is at noon" when I ate. And the pain. My sensitivity to light was so strong that I had to wear sunglasses all the time, even at night. Something that I clearly took for granted was gone.

However, as much as I went through physically, the spiritual awakening I experienced superseded it all. Although I could not see, I saw. God revealed himself to me on a deeper level and gave me glimpses of who HE created me to be. The visions played in my mind, like the coming attractions to a movie. I saw myself speaking in front of people. I saw myself sitting at a table repeatedly signing my name. It became obvious to me that my childhood affinities for writing and the creative arts and sciences were clues to my purpose, my destiny. So, after my sight was restored one would think that I would hit the ground running, chasing destiny, right? Wrong!

You see, when butterflies first emerge, they have to wait for several hours before they can fly. This is the very moment in which I often get stuck and tripped up. In the stillness of waiting, my mind would become weighed down with self-defeating thoughts of doubt, worry, the "am I really good enough?" syndrome, and once again, fear. So much to the point, I would start questioning if I heard from God and heard Him correctly. Hence, the reason I metaphorically have emerged as a butterfly and have not soared to my fullest potential.

But thanks be to God that He doesn't just give us revelations, He sends confirmations. In my case, there have been instances God had to send confirmation after confirmation and then some more confirmations. They would come through godsends such as sermons, songs, bumper stickers, and people, giving me the little reminders and encouragement that I needed to move forward. God would even "show up and show out" in some of the most unexpected places.

For instance, I remember being at a casting call with a director who specialized in the film and television industry. Before the auditioning process began, he posed a question to us and asked "if you could be successful in one area only, would you chose film, television, or theater" and we had to explain why. The question sent me into a tailspin. Instead of studying the script, I was feeling the effects of "an inner battle." But, when it was my turn to answer, I wanted a job, so I was prepared to say film. However, my inner butterfly found her voice and said, "theater, because that's my ministry." Then I wondered to myself, "who said that?" The director put his paper down and for the next 15 minutes he spoke into my life. Although I heard the director's voice, I knew it was God speaking to me. Once again, I was being reminded that He who started a good work in me was going to see it to completion. After the audition I found myself getting involved in several drama ministries that fueled the "theater buff" in me. The opportunities I had to write plays and skits led to me writing inspirational articles and the start of an inspirational greeting card line. A year later I even secured a role as an extra in an inspirational film of which the same director was a part. This was definitely a full circle moment and I was on a roll.

As time passed I was not only being stretched creatively but spiritually. The notion of "there has to be more to life than this" began to invade my thoughts and resulted in some restless and sleepless nights. Naturally, this caused me to do some deeper soul searching, as some leaps of faith were on the horizon. And we know how scary those can be.

During one of my quiet moments, I reflected on the "out of the comfort zone feeling" a caterpillar must experience as it spins its cocoon in an upside down position. Then it came to mind how taxing and tiring the process must be and yet the caterpillar keeps spinning toward its destiny. Meaning that I, too, had to keep going in spite of my feelings, my circumstances and situations, disappointments, setbacks, being misunderstood, the nay-sayers, the fear, my insecurities, or whatever arose and tried to discourage me. I had to keep pressing toward the mark of my higher calling.

Then a fact I knew for years finally seeped into the depth of my soul and clicked. I began to meditate on how a caterpillar already has (in capital letters) the specialized cells it needs to become a butterfly. "The click" was so pronounced that it silenced all the would've, could've and should've thoughts that haunted my now, 41-year-old self.

After praying and seeking guidance, I was lead to pursue an advanced degree in Public Health that awarded a certificate in health education and promotion. The course of study provided the perfect balance between my love for the arts and sciences. This was truly a leap of faith, considering the 19-year lapse since my last degree. Despite the challenges I faced to get back into the academic swing of things, it was this leap that connected some lingering dots in my life and made my heart's desires tangible. One of them being the inspirational greeting card line I spoke about earlier.

Anyone that knows me could attest to how much I adore inspirational greeting cards because of the power they have to encourage others. So, I got my plan together, invested in a trademark (of a butterfly of course), and secured a business certificate. The verses were written, the designs were planned out, and my line of postcards were printed. Although, I did manage to get them sold in various local Christian bookstores, the venture did not take off like I had hoped and it was very costly at that. Needless to say, I became discouraged and stopped printing the postcards. But, every now and then, a verse of inspiration would hit me in the wee hours of the night causing me to keep a pen and paper handy. I eventually started doing small runs of holiday cards for family and friends. In retrospect, I know this was God helping me keep my dream alive for a bigger plan to manifest. So here it is fifteen years later, and I would have never imagined that the cards would be used as a fundraising venture to support community organizations that empower children, teens, and women. Once again reminding me it's never too late and not to give up on my dreams. And God didn't stop there, as more dots began to connect.

In March of 2013, the vision I had of me signing my name repeatedly came into fruition at the book signing of my first children's book. This road was definitely one of perseverance and endurance. But just like the caterpillar, I kept spinning toward my destiny in the midst of multiple rejection letters from publishing companies and facing my biggest hurdle, which was financing the project, after I decided to self-publish. But I took a leap of faith and set up the date for the first installment to be drafted from my account without knowing how it or the rest of them were going to be paid. Although I had to make some sacrifices along the way, God definitely favored me and made ways out of no way, on multiple levels. Even the obstacles I faced after the book was published were miraculously remedied from the support of my mother, family and friends, and countless godsends. I soon found myself speaking in front of people doing workshops, seminars, and panel discussions. Oh wait, I can't forget about my theater background that "set the stage" for me to successfully bring my book to life in schools.

Overall, each of these successes were long-awaited manifestations that laid the foundation for my current-day entrepreneurial pursuits. The trademark and company I established years ago is now an organization that inspires clients to discover, embrace, and celebrate their unique gifts, talents, and abilities, using the creative arts and sciences as tools of empowerment. The exact ones that empowered me. And as the saying goes, God is not through with me yet!

So, as my destiny continues to unfold, so does the relationship with my father. It's been a year since we met and the bond between us is strengthening, as God continues to work in and through this situation. And it all started with a leap of faith and has thus far worked out for my good.

Moving forward, I know there are many more leaps of faith to come and I am excited. For as the Bible says, I am fearfully and wonderfully made. It also says, that I am created for a purpose. But most importantly it says, *"I know the plans I have for you,"* declares the LORD, *"plans to prosper you and not to harm you, plans to give you hope and a future. So, here I am Lord, I am ready to soar!"*

ABOUT

Bweela Steptoe

Bweela Steptoe walks the creative realm with ease. She is the daughter of two very different artists and tells her story through the designs she creates. Her father, the illustrator John Steptoe, gained fame in the 70s and 80s for his children's books. Bweela's mother, Stephanie Douglas, is a collagist and painter whose work speaks to the richness of her urban experience.

Bweela Steptoe's rags-to-riches style aims to express a kind of inner city resourcefulness she calls "Urban Deconstruction." Steptoe enjoys creating one-of-kind garments and she also enjoys creating the fabric she uses in her designs. Bweela uses her artistic background and family art influences as an inspiration for her fabric and clothing designs. The splashes and footprints that embellish her deconstructed garments are a defiant reminder of where she came from and, for that matter, where she wants to go. The designer's strong views on how women project themselves are expressed through the clothing she presents. She feels that today's woman can be very sexy — and yet still leave something to the imagination.

Bweela is a graduate of The Fashion Institute of Technology, where she received degrees in Accessory and Knitwear Design. At FIT, Bweela acquired knowledge in all aspects of the fashion industry. Since graduating, Bweela has been designing for private clients, as well as selling out of several small boutiques in New York City, including locations in Brooklyn, where the designer also resides.

View and purchase her designs, contact the designer and find out more about her work.

Website: www.bweelasteptoe.com
            http://shopvida.com/collections/bweela-steptoe
Facebook: Bweela.steptoe.1
LinkedIn: Bweela Steptoe

A MOTHER'S LOVE AND FIGHT FOR HER DAUGHTERS

by Bweela Steptoe

Driving back home after dropping one of my twin daughters, Ayanna, off to begin her second year in Savannah College of Arts & Design (SCAD) in Georgia, I thought about how I could change my life so I could change my financial situation. I would often ask myself, why is it that I am a 46-year-old talented fashion designer and still struggling financially? I guess having two daughters in private colleges was a part of it. Just to get both of them back in school for the fall semester was difficult. However, on that drive I kept thinking to myself that it just shouldn't have to be this way.

It was September 14 and it was also my father's birthday. My dad was the late John Lewis Steptoe, an award-winning author and illustrator of children's books. He would have been 66 years old. Just a few weeks earlier, I had a street co-naming event where my father's childhood street, Monroe Street in Brooklyn New York, was co-named John Lewis Steptoe Place. It was a three-year task that I had finally achieved with the help and support of many wonderful people. Although this was a great achievement, I knew that were many other great goals and aspirations that I planned to achieve in my lifetime. I was blessed enough to have two parents who were both artists. They met in Art and Design High School. It was hard to believe that my father left a great legacy for my brother and me and there I was driving back home with no money trying to figure out how I'm I going to pay for my daughters' school this year. Yes, I was blessed enough for both of them to get scholarships, as well as assistance from other outside agencies, but because they are both in private out-of-state colleges it is way more expensive than a state university would be.

When Ayanna and Asha were young, we were told that they both had a learning disability. I never could understand how or why because they initially appeared to be comprehending and understanding what they were being taught. I've even had my friends tell me they don't look like they have a learning disability! But what does a kid look like when they have a learning disability? They both always loved books and reading. I've purchased books requested by them every Christmas as gifts practically since their birth. I would read them stories every night before bed, just as my father did with me and my brother. They would also write their own stories. A lot of the times Ayanna would draw the pictures and Asha would make up the story. In pre-K, they would get perfect scores on their spelling tests.

It wasn't until they went to the first grade that they began to have problems. They would have problems spelling words and have problems with the concept of the value of numbers. When I spoke to their teachers about it they would say that they would grow out of it. I didn't really feel comfortable with that answer. But I went along with it. When they were in second grade I saw that they were having more difficulty. I remember having conversations with their teachers. They would tell me not to worry about it. But I was worried about it because doing homework had become torture. They used to cry, fight, kick, and scream. It wasn't fun for me or them, to say the least.

By the end of second grade I knew I had to do something as their teachers were talking about holding my daughters back! I didn't think that it was the right thing to do. Why should they repeat the same grade again? I had to take control of the situation and create the destiny that I wanted for my daughters! I couldn't take what someone else said just like that. The issue of them learning and the way they learned needed to be addressed. Not having them repeat the same thing over again. So I decided to get them tested and find out what was going on. After having them tested I was told that they both had a learning disability. They both had difficulty with comprehension and the concept of numbers on different levels. I was told that math and reading are connected in the brain. So if you have difficulties with math you might have comprehension issues as well. It was all hard for me to absorb.

I was told that I needed to get the girls an IEP which is an Individual Educational Plan so they could get the extra support that they need in class. However, this situation does not always work for every child. We tried it for a while and, just like I thought, it really didn't work for them. In addition to the extra help in the classroom, they went to school thirty minutes before class started as well as doing after-school tutoring. Although they were improving, it was still really hard for them and they were still behind. Eventually we put both of them into private school and their whole attitude changed. They were actually were happy to get up and go to school every morning and were doing a lot better.

But it still wasn't easy for me. I had a long way to go dealing with the Board of Education. You have to know that having your child in a private school makes a large difference in the way that they are taught. If you don't win your case with the Board of Ed., you risk the chance of having to pay for the school yourself. It was always in the back of my mind every time it was time to go to a hearing and deal with the Board of Ed. Making sure that you comply with all of their rules and regulations. My job as a mother was to make sure that my children got a proper education. So if it meant suing the Board of Ed every year until my daughters were finished with their high school, then that's what I would do. I did it every year. It wasn't easy.

Fast forward and now Asha's in her second year at Johnson and Wales in Rhode Island and Ayanna is in her second year at SCAD. As I drove back I thought about what I needed to do as a responsible parent to make sure that my girls could stay in these top private colleges. With only two more years to go, I couldn't give up now. But what could I do? That's when I said to myself, "Hey, hello, Bweela! You have a father who left you a legacy!" You see, for years after my father's death I was told that I should only look at my inheritance as dessert. I was made to feel that I shouldn't really try to exploit it or use it to build on. Or for that matter, depend on it to live off of. I thought to myself that here I have something wonderful that was left for me to share with the world and to do with as I please and I was always made to feel otherwise. It was left to me for me to be able to live off of! To make my life better! To make my life easier! To make my children's lives better so that I could spend time with them and be the proper parent. My father always said to me, "Make sure that you have enough money so that you can stay home and raise your children. Don't be in a position where you have to work and have someone else raise your children." His work is the legacy that I am supposed to build on! He set this up for my brother and me so our lives could be easier than his was. Isn't that what a lot of people do for their children? I needed to use what I had to take care of myself as well as my children. At that point I realized that I could no longer live in the shadow of someone else's fear!

One of the many books that my father wrote and illustrated, called Mufaro's Beautiful Daughters, which is an African tale that is similar to a Cinderella story, was adapted into a play. It's currently on a nationwide tour for a third season. I have the ability to sell John Steptoe merchandise during the public performances of Mufaro's Beautiful Daughters! The fact that this story still has a shelf life after nearly 30 years in publication is a blessing in itself. I'm going to make money from what I already have to ensure that my daughters get the education that they deserve and have fought so hard for so many years.

This has been a long journey and struggle! Yet it did not have to be so. Or maybe it did in order for me to respect and cherish who I am and what I have. I won't have to keep struggling in pain. I don't have to keep putting myself through financial hardship when I have the golden egg. I remember my daughter Asha asking me a month or two after she finally started attending private school why did I take so long to put her in private school? I told her I didn't know. But I also told her that I was afraid because I didn't have the money to pay for school if the Board of Ed. denied me? I would have to pay out of my pocket for the $40,000 school tuition for school times two! I didn't have that kind of money! Nevertheless, this journey taught me that you have to believe that you are going to win and you will win every single time. No matter how hard it is. No matter how many obstacles come your way. No matter how much work you have to put in. You do what you have to do! It works out. It might not always work out exactly the way you think it will. It might not be the way you planned but it will. But it works out as long as you believe that it will!

ABOUT
Terryl Ebony

Terryl Ebony is an empowerment speaker, life & business strategist, author, and community activist. Terryl is the CEO/President of Find Your Purpose. She serves clients through coaching, speaking engagements, and professional development, helping them to find meaningful strategies to navigate a holistic lifestyle in the direct areas of personal, business, and parenting.

Terryl authored "Losing Love, Having Faith, & Finding Hope," which is centered on everyday parent/child issues and developments she experienced while raising her son. Terryl offers profound coaching advice to parents that find themselves going through similar situations.

Terryl founded "The Misunderstood Youth Development Center," a non-profit organization whose mission is to help understand, develop, and stimulate the minds of our youth. The organization mentors and counsels young men ages 14-19 that have criminal court involvement.

Terryl hopes that, from her experiences and words, she is able to touch someone's heart and mind, creating a positive transformation from within. It is her expectation that through these self-revelations a better person, family, and community will result.

For more information on Terryl Ebony,
visit her website at **www.terrylebony.com**.

She can also be found on all social media
platforms **@terrylebony**.

WHEN I STOPPED PLAYING DOUBLE DUTCH

By Terryl Ebony

Growing up, I loved to play double-dutch. I couldn't wait to go outside during my lunch period or to get home because I knew it was double-dutch time. I would think about all the different tricks I would do while I was in rope, or how long I would be able to jump. I even knew how to jump scotch, which is really just backwards double-dutch. The best feeling was when there was a battle because I could really show off my talents. Double-dutch was my safe haven, that thing I was really good at and no one could take that from me. However, that wasn't always the case. When I first learned how to jump, I was very intimidated. I was scared of the rope and even more scared of the people watching me jump the rope. I just knew when I jumped in the rope would smack me in the face. I also knew if I jumped in at the wrong time, I would trip and fall. Then I would be embarrassed because everyone would laugh at me, and who likes to be laughed at? Not me! So what did I do? I chose not to learn how to jump. Instead, I learned how to turn. I became the block and school double-dutch turner. I sat idle and watched everyone have fun jumping, while my hands were tired from turning.

One day, that all changed. There were only three of us outside, and of course, I was turning so the other two girls could jump. One of the girls kept nudging me to try it. She kept asking, "What do you have to lose?" She didn't know about all the anxiety and other reasons going through my head. She didn't understand what I was going through because she already knew how to jump. It was easy for her. I didn't quite see it that way. But, for whatever reason, on this day she was a bit more persistent than usual. It didn't seem like she was buying any of my excuses that day, and I was honestly getting tired of saying no and making excuses. So I took a chance and said, "Ok." I won't lie to you, I was a nervous wreck! I was scared out of mind! She showed me the rhythm the rope should have before I get in and the key signs to look for. It all made sense because I had been watching people jump in the rope for at least a year now. However, her coaching and pep talks didn't ease my tension. I was still afraid, almost to the point of paralysis. I did not want this rope to hit me in the face. I did not want to fall; but, most importantly, I did not want to fail.

Against my better judgment, I closed my eyes as tight as I could, put my hands over my face, and I went for it. Exactly what I thought, the rope hit me in the face and I messed up. Although that disappointed me, I was happier knowing no one laughed at me and I didn't feel embarrassed. They gave me another chance; so I closed my eyes, covered my face, and I went for it again. The same thing happened. Now, I'm starting to get frustrated and I wanted to give up. That's when my friend said, "Terryl, you might actually make it in the rope if you could SEE the rope." So, of course, I gave her the side eye – "Miss Know-It-All," but I reluctantly tried it. I timed the rope's rhythm; I had one foot in and one foot out the rope. At some point I had to make the decision when to jump in. I gave it a lot of thought, after about a good five minutes I went for it, and guess what? It worked! I got in and took a few steps. I probably would have jumped longer but I remember screaming and laughing so hard that I just stopped and dropped to the ground. I couldn't believe I did it. Not only did I do it, I couldn't believe that it wasn't as hard as I thought it would be. And from that moment on, I jumped, I turned, and I did unimaginable tricks. You could not stop me, all because I took a leap of faith, faced my fears, and made a decision to do it.

Fast forward a few years, I found myself regressing back to those double-dutch days. Now I'm older; I have a child; no college education; but, a lot of ideas. So many things I wanted to do, so many great concepts floating around in that brain of mine. However, with each vision came fear and doubt, which led to procrastination and stagnation. I second-guessed every step of progression. I went back to the days of not thinking I was good enough, that no one would believe in me, no one would support me, no one would think that I was capable or smart enough – after all I was considered uneducated without that college paper. So many people told me that having a child at such a young age was like a death sentence for a prosperous career and life. So many people said working a city job or a 9 to 5 with a pension was the best way to go. So many people had such negative things to say. Now, don't get me wrong, I did have some people in my corner that were cheering me on, but I won't lie – the negative stuff somehow sounded more convincing and easier to digest. So I started to believe it too. It was easy to believe that I couldn't, I wouldn't, and I shouldn't. After all, who was I to believe I could defy all odds? Who was I to believe that the idea of becoming an entrepreneur could actually become a reality? Who was I to believe that I would some-day become a published author or that I could be an international speaker who inspires the world to fulfill their dreams?

I was the person that suffered internally and quietly with self-doubt and fear day after day, week after week, and month after month. It was too important for others to see the brave, tough girl that endured all things. It was too important for me to prove everyone wrong. I was so frustrated because I knew I was standing in my own way, blocking my blessings. I began to think to myself, "There has got to be a better way." Life is not supposed to be this challenging. Right? Why am I waking up every day wanting more, knowing I'm unhappy, unsatisfied, and unfulfilled? I knew I was in such a rut, but I did nothing about it. Until the day I had a conversation with God and He told me the only person I had to prove something to was myself. There was something in the moment that clicked. There was something in that moment that made me believe I could do all things through Christ that strengthens me. There was something in that moment that made me care less about my fears, less about what others thought, and more about what I had to offer the world. I was also tired of being fired or quitting jobs because I needed to be there for my son. I knew in my heart that a 9 to 5 was not my calling. I had to create my own hours, my own money, my own destiny, and my own opportunities.

So in 2005, I took a leap of faith and started the non-profit organization called The Misunderstood Youth Development Center (MYDC). I had no idea how to run a non-profit. I didn't know any of the laws or rules, but I did know there were a lot of young people that needed the services I wanted to provide. So, I asked questions; I researched; I read books and I networked. I did what was necessary to get the organization established, running, and relevant to the youth and parents in the community. Today, MYDC helps young men charged with low level felonies get their charges sealed and dismissed, or at the very least reduced, after undergoing an intense 12-month program of individual and group counseling, substance education, critical and consequential thinking, training, and much more. MYDC also provides development classes for parents ordered by the court to receive counseling in order to be reconnected with their children.

After witnessing and speaking to so many youths and parents over the years, I realized how much of the turmoil with our young people began at home. I realized how clueless many parents were about how their actions were truly affecting their children. I recognized it because it happened in my own home, under my nose, and it took me a while to figure it out. When I did, I thought it would be a good idea to tell my story to others so they could learn something from it. If I could save one child from going through some of the hurt and pain that I witnessed with my son, I wanted to do that. So, once again, I knew nothing about writing a book, but I knew this story needed to be told. In 2013, "Losing Love, Having Faith, & Finding Hope" was published. Who would have thought that I could be a published author? I know I didn't. It took me a few years to publish it because old habits die hard, and I went back to playing double-dutch, doubting my story was good enough, fearing I wouldn't help anyone or sell any books. At the end of 2012, I remember making the commitment to myself that I would not let another year pass by without publishing my book. I would not be afraid to tell a story that could have such a positive effect on people and possibly change the outcome of a little boy or little girl's life, not to mention the relationship of a family overall.

That year, I also completed so much of the educational goals that I had. First, I received credentialing as a Family Development Supervisor. Next, I got my CASAC-T, which stands for Credentialed Alcohol and Substance Abuse Counselor in Training. Finally, I received my degree in Human Services from the University of Phoenix. I don't know how I got through it all, but I kept saying I can do all things through Christ that strengthens me. I was finally getting to a place where I truly believed in myself. I didn't need or seek anyone's approval. I no longer had one foot in the rope and one foot out. Both feet were planted on solid ground. I was now playing to WIN!

In 2015, the position of New York State Assembly opened up in my community. I was not sure at the time why God told me to run this race, but he did and I obeyed. I knew this could be another way to effect great change and I'm all for that. I also knew it would be a longshot for me to win because I was considered the underdog. I didn't make the ballot because my opponent challenged my signatures. Everyone thought I would give up and that would be that. However, giving up is not really something that I do very easily. So, I continued to run but not because I really thought I could win. I ran because it was important for the community to understand how the electoral process really works. Many people didn't know what went on behind the scenes. My race now became the eyes and ears for the community. I chose to use my candidacy as a platform to educate the uneducated. So, although I didn't win the position, I was absolutely victorious in my mission.

Nowadays, I use my platform to speak and coach others on how to fulfill their dreams and find their purpose. I mainly work with entrepreneurs, business owners, and corporate leaders, equipping them with the necessary systems, processes, and strategies to increase their productivity and bottom line. When I first started out, I was very intimidated by all the other coaches and experts in the field. Again, I started to backslide into the world of "I'm not good enough." Thankfully, this time it didn't last long, mainly due to all my past successes. I am comfortable and confident in letting the world know that I am good enough. I am more than a conqueror. I am a designer's original, and no one can do what I do, like I do. That is what makes me stand apart in my field, with my clients. My test has become my testimony and all the mess I've been through is now the message I can share proudly with the world. Looking back at everything I've been through and all that I've accomplished, I sometimes ask myself, "What would have happened if I had still been playing double-dutch, if I still had one foot in the rope and one foot out, if I still kept doubting myself and looking for the approval of others? Where would I be today?"

With that in mind, there is no reason for you not to pursue your dreams. There is no reason for you not to find your purpose. There is no reason for you to continue doing the same thing day after day, week after week, and year after year and not produce the results you want. That is insane! You have to make a commitment to yourself today to stop playing double-dutch, stop having one foot in the rope and one foot out, stop second guessing yourself, stop telling yourself you're not good enough, not pretty enough, not worthy enough, or not smart enough. Change that thought in your head that says you're going to fail, that you can't write that book, that you can't start that business, or that no one is going to like your product or service. Change that thought that says you have to stay in that failed or abusive relationship. Change that thought that says you can't lose weight, or you can't get that GED or college degree. Just change the conversation. Start by telling yourself that you, too, will be able to do all things through Christ that strengths you. Know that you are good enough and if God has given you a talent, no one can take that away. Don't doubt yourself; believe in what's already inside of you. Dedicate time to working on yourself, your craft, and your passions. Commit to going the distance and not giving up. The things we want to achieve may not come easily, but they will come and at the end of the day, just remember to give God the glory. You can do this!

ABOUT

Elizabeth M Johnson EA, CB

Elizabeth is a practicing Enrolled Agent and Professional Bookkeeper who graduated from Northeastern University with a B.S.B.A in Accounting and Finance. After working in the accounting and tax departments of many large corporations in the Boston Area, Elizabeth started her own practice, specializing in accounting for small to midsize businesses 10 years ago. EMJ is a three-year member of the National Association of Tax Professionals (NATP), National Society of Accountants (NSA), and a five-year member of American Institute of Professional Bookkeepers (AIPB).

Elizabeth focus is on improving clients' long-term growth, profitability, and tax savings, without sacrificing financial stability.

Over 50% of her clients have become self-made millionaires due to their hard work and her financial and tax advice. She believes, it's not what you make but what you keep.

Elizabeth is a wife to a loving husband Tyron for 11 years and a mom of four wonderful children-Jaylen, 11, Nevaeh and Daniel, 9, and Sarai, 6, and lives in Weymouth MA.

Website:	www.emjfinancialservices.com
Facebook	emjfinancial
Twitter	@emjfinancial @mstaxstrategist
Linked In:	linkedin.com/in/elizabeth-johnson-7a827b11
Instagram:	emjfinancial_
Adsress:	775 Pleasant Street Ste 3 E. Weymouth MA 02189 Ph: 781-340-1829 Fax: 781-340-1829

Help Simplify Your Financial Life by Making Sense of Your Money!

WOUNDED BUT NOT DESTROYED

Elizabeth M Johnson EA, CB

I remember the day like it was yesterday. In July of 2009, I received some devastating news from my full-time employer. I was getting laid off. Three months later my husband was also laid off from his job. Adding to our stress, in between our two layoffs, we found out that we were pregnant with our fourth child. And if that wasn't enough, the doctor called back two weeks after I had taken the pregnancy test to tell us that our baby might have Down syndrome and a hole in her heart. At this point, without being aware, it brought my husband and me closer than ever before. We were going through so much and just knew was that we had to be there to strengthen and pray for each other.

We went from making over $100,000 in combined annual income to less than $45,000 annually in combined unemployment. All we could think about was how we were going to pay the mortgage, car notes, and insurance on two cars, and take care of a four children with less than half of the income that we had before. After struggling for two months, my husband and I decided that we had to move. But the only way to move was to file for bankruptcy. I just thought and prayed about this situation over and over. Thoughts like, "How does an accountant file bankruptcy? And how does someone with a BA in not only accounting, but finance, file bankruptcy?" We were fortunate to have met an attorney who walked us through the foreclosure process, free of charge. We were able to stay in our home for a whole year without having to pay the mortgage. So we saved everything we could, because we knew the day would come when we would have to move. On the exact same day we went to court for the foreclosure and the bank gave us a move-out date, we also found an apartment nearby. Because the apartment was move-in ready, and we wanted to move before our baby was born. We asked the mortgage company if they would give us money for the keys if we moved out sooner. And they said yes. So we got more money to return the keys to the bank and it helped us with the first, last, and security deposit we needed. Although we were going through our trials it was so hard to not see God in what was happening and because we saw him, we decided to be thankful.

We were able to move, unpack, and get settled before our fourth child, who we named Sarai, was born. On June 9, 2010, I had a scheduled Cesarean, due to complications with my first pregnancy, and because I gave birth to twins during my second pregnancy. I was told that I had to have the same procedure as the prior two for safety reasons. But this time was even more nerve-racking. Not only was I nervous about being cut for the third time in the same area on my stomach, but I was nervous about finding out if Sarai was going to be a Down syndrome baby as the doctor had stated at the beginning of my pregnancy. However, because we decided that we would accept her as she was, regardless of how she turned out, when the doctor offered me to take the test to see if she was a Downs syndrome baby, I declined. At little after 11am, Sarai was born, a healthy baby. She was not diagnosed as having Down syndrome nor did she have a hole in her heart. My husband and I just cried. Our faith was upheld and our prayers were answered. What seemed like a curse at the time was actually a blessing and this was just the beginning. But, of course, my eyes were not opened to this realization until about three years ago.

Two years prior to getting laid off, I started my part-time tax business. I was only doing taxes for family and friends and only I had about 25 clients. The year I got laid off my clientele doubled to 50. In 2010, my clientele doubled to 100. By 2012 I was servicing over 150 clients and decided that I could no longer complete tax returns in my home. Nervous at the thought of moving into an office and paying expenses for upkeep, I did much praying. In October 2012, I moved into my first office rental space in Hanover, Massachusetts, paying $300.00 a month rent which included utilities. This was such an answered prayer. By 2014, I had grown out of my Hanover office space and needed a larger office space. I was now servicing over 300 clients. So, in early 2014, I moved to my second office. My rent more than doubled because of the size and location of the space. I was not only closer to Boston but my new office space was located in an historical mansion in Randolph, MA. I fell in love with this new space from the very first time

I went to see it and so did all my clients that came to visit. The landlord wanted to rent it for $250.00 more than what I ended up paying. You ask how I did that; my answer, "I didn't," I prayed and went to my God and told him what I wanted to pay and he gave me just that!

Loving my second location much more than the first, I wanted to stay there forever. But that was not God's plan for me. My God whose name is Jesus did it again. You see, by 2015, I had over 600 tax clients and a portfolio of 100 bookkeeping clients. I was now making the six figures I had always dreamed of making. My dreams were coming to life by the minute.

Fast forward seven years later and I just closed on a two-story office condo. I am on my way to making seven figures annually. And we are still in the same apartment that we moved into in 2010. We are looking for our dream home and we are also looking for land to possibly build our dream home. Whichever road the Lord tells to take, we will follow. Never in a million years would I have thought I would be where I am today. But the bible says, "If ye have faith as a grain of mustard seed, nothing shall be impossible unto you (Matthew 17:20)," and that is all we had. I wrote down what I wanted and put it in my bible. Every now and then, I would read over the list and was so happy to be able to cross something off because that goal was met.

Today, I am here to tell you that I was wounded but I was not destroyed. It was not an easy road but every hurdle that I had to jump and mountain I had to climb was worth it. You see, during the times that my business was being blessed, my household was suffering. Because I was working so many hours each day, seven days a week at times, my relationship with my husband suffered. I was barely home to spend that quality time with him anymore and because I was working late nights and on weekends my children barely saw me. My mom, mother-in law, and husband had to come together to do the things that I was not there to do. At times, this made me feel really sad because I was not being the "mommy" my children needed me to be. So, here I was again in between crossroads; completely opposite from where I was three to five years ago. I had a successful business and was in a much better financial position but it all came at the cost of spending time with my family. I knew this could not continue for too much longer. I knew I had to make some changes to balance my roles as a mom, wife, and businesswoman. I always told my children I am mom first but I was not showing it. I would make promises to my husband and set up dinner dates and have to cancel at the last minute because I was too tired from the long day. They wanted to be happy about the continued growth of the business but they didn't know how to do that and share with me how they needed me more. The turning point for me was when my oldest sat me down one morning and told me that he had stopped telling me things that was happening at his school because he said I was going to be too busy to make it. Even though I never missed a teacher's meeting, field trip, field day, concert, or project for any of my four children, my oldest, Jaylen, felt guilty for asking me to take time away from work to be with him. I cried so much. I did not my want my babies feeling like they came second to my career. So, you know what I did? I prayed. I asked the Lord to make a way for me to balance my life. I needed equilibrium. I didn't want to feel my left side heavier than my right side nor my right side heavier than my left anymore. I wanted to be there for my family and my business. It was not until this year did I find this balance. My answer from the Lord was for Tyron, my husband, and I to work together. I have to admit, I didn't grasp this idea right away. I didn't know how it was going to be working with my husband every day and then going home with him. I was nervous for our relationship. The other reasons were because our medical benefits were with his job and the thought of all our income coming from EMJ Financial Services was exciting and daunting at the same time. In 2015, I finally had the talk with my husband and shared with him what the Lord had told me. Unlike my first reaction, he welcomed the thought and was on board. I told him, we can do it, but let's wait two years and then you can give your notice. But God said "NO"! The time was not two years from now but the time was now. Tyron had worked for an alternative school in Boston. He had worked there for a little over five years as a culinary teacher. This summer, he gave his notice and now we work together. My eyes are watering as I am writing this. These are tears of joy, of course. As I can't tell you how much burden has been lifted off of us since we started working together. We are happier and our children Jaylen, Nevaeh, Daniel, and Sarai are happier. The shift was immediate. I was so angry at myself for pushing this off because I thought it was going to be difficult. I could have delayed a few grays if I had been obedient the first time around. However, I do thank God for his grace and mercy and not leaving me for being disobedient. Tyron is not the only one that works for EMJ now. I now have a personal administrative assistant, three bookkeepers, and another tax professional. This all happened in a matter of nine months. I went from having one bookkeeper and myself to now having six, including Tyron. My business is now sufficient for the work we have and the "new" work that is soon to come. What I once dreamt has come to life, what I once spoke has come to existence. I am frequently reminded of the time I worked as a research assistant at my mom's job the summer after high school. I remember telling all the ladies that I worked with, that were all older than me, that I was not going to work for someone all my life. I told them that I was going to own my own business. One of the ladies, Mary, chimed in and told me that when I do start my business, I need to hire her. We all laughed but meant every word. Mary found me on Facebook several months ago through mutual friends. She sent me a friend request and I accepted. She then sent me a private message and told me to send her a job application. I smiled from ear to ear. She remembered, what I had told her over 16 years ago. She told me how proud she was that I kept my word and I stayed focused and accomplished what I said I was going to do. I told her that I had a support system so tight that it would have been a sin to not take on the opportunities that presented themselves. I always worked hard while staying humble and I know this attitude has helped me get to where I am now.

My biggest life lessons came in the midst of financial devastation. Nevertheless, it's through my experience that I found my footing in the world as an accountant and enrolled agent who educates, consults, and witnesses to those who are now struggling in the same way that I had. I let them know that it does get better. I am here to tell you that you may be wounded now, or have been wounded, but in no way are you destroyed because, "With God All Things Are Possible," Matthew 19:26). So remember, "Work for a cause, not for applause. Live life to express and not to impress. Don't strive to make your presence noticed, make your absence felt. Work hard and stay humble."

See you at the top!

Elizabeth Johnson, EA

ABOUT
Rachel Lopez Evans

Rachel believes that everyone has pivotal moments that changes one's life and direction, and she's had many, too many to count. After being enrolled in the military by her mother, two failed marriages, single parenting, and failing health; Rachel was disillusioned with love and life. Ironically, every setback, obstacle, challenge, and struggle only pivoted her towards triumph. The military offered salvation and opportunity for Rachel, who retired from the military with a Master's Degree after 21 years of honorable service. After the military, Rachel changed direction again when she became a real estate investor, a network marketer, a photographer, and now a health coach. As a health coach, Rachel feels that it was her calling to offer a greater service to women facing health challenges, like she once did. Rachel has one daughter who has grown up to become a journalist and is working on her first novel.

Facebook:	BoomingHealth4Life
	IamRLEvans
IG:	R.L. Evans
	BoomingHealth4Life
Twitter:	@booming_health

CHARITIES AND CAUSES THAT ARE IMPORTANT TO RACHEL AND THAT SHE SUPPORTS:

Breast Cancer

http://www.projectrenewalgeorgia.com :
a Domestic Violence Intervention Program changing lives in Rockdale, Newton, and Walton Counties

LEAPING INTO MY DESTINY

By Rachel Lopez Evans

If there is one thing that I've learned it's that every setback is a set-up for an opportunity to come back. When I was 17 years old, six months before I graduated high school, my mother signed me up for the Army. My siblings and I sat at the dinner table doing our homework and my mother was at the stove cooking dinner. She stopped cooking, turned to me, and said, "Tomorrow when you get out of school, I need you to go to the recruiting station and sign some documents. You're going into the Army when you graduate." My brother and my sister looked at each other in utter amazement. She then turned to look at me with that "look" and I replied, "Yes, ma'am." You see, we had the type of mother that ruled with an iron fist and whatever she says, goes. Six months later, exactly one month after I graduated high school, at 5:00 in the morning, three Army recruiters came and escorted me out of my home in New York City. So, I didn't make the choice to join the Army, the choice was made for me, but what I made of that choice was the most important lesson I learned. Oh, yes, I've had bumps and bruises along the way, but they only made me stronger and more determined to succeed in life.

Serving my country nearly cost me my freedom and almost got me locked up in prison. You see, I made the stupid mistake of doctoring "secret" documents in order to protect someone I loved. This someone happened to be my husband. Needless to say, my superiors caught me. My husband was caught too. His punishment was a dishonorable discharge and mine could have been the maximum punishment, which was to be reduced in all ranks and locked up in military prison. The chain of command must have had pity on me because at the time of my punishment I was six months pregnant. So instead, I received the punishment of a reduction of two grades, forfeiture of pay for two months, and extra duty for 45 days. Needless to say, our lifestyle took a drastic change. We went from driving a Porsche and a BMW to driving a second-hand car. We went from living in a huge three- bedroom apartment to living in a one- bedroom closet. We went from having two paychecks to living on half of one paycheck. My career in the military appeared to be over. My supervisors were trying to convince me to just get out. But where would we go? My family was in no condition to take in a couple and a baby. I had no education past high school and neither did my husband.

I felt my world was crumbling in around me. I found myself in a foreign country, with no support from family or friends. I was about to have a baby, and to make matters worse, my marriage was crumbling. The only comfort I found was in prayer. I prayed every single night, and every single waking moment. Prayers were a form of meditation for me. It gave me hope that something better was just around the corner. It finally came in the form of my beautiful baby girl. In the middle of all the chaos and turmoil that was going on in my career, my marriage, and in my life, my daughter gave me something positive on which to focus. She made me feel like I had a purpose in life and that I needed to work on me so that she can have a better future.

So I enrolled in college. Back then, there were no online courses in existence. So, I had to physically go to a classroom after working 10 hours a day. My daughter was small enough that I was able to take her to class with me in a baby seat. Thankfully, she was a quiet baby and never made a peep while I was in class. I would wake up every single morning at 5:00 and participate in the Army physical fitness program that consisted of various exercises and running up to five or ten miles. Then I would go home and fix breakfast for us, go to work all day, and be in a classroom at night. By the time I would get home it would be 10:00 in the evening and I would have to start this process all over again the next day. This went on for several years. In the midst of this, I found myself separated from my husband and barely making it on my own on the low income I was making in the military. I started to find creative ways to generate income and put food in my daughter's stomach, even if this meant I would not eat. I would purchase items on credit from the military store and return it the next day for cash. Unfortunately, I found myself having to sell contraband items to the local Germans. Again, praying got me through these hard times. Selling contraband is a serious violation that could have landed me jail time and a dishonorable discharge from the military.

Soon, my military career began to progress, which increased my income. I was finally earning the income I needed to stop the illegal selling of contraband. Everything in my life was moving towards a positive direction. But, just as there are no straight roads to any one destination, there certainly weren't any in my life. My heart was literally torn in half when I went to pick up my daughter from the babysitter only to find that she had been abused. She had bruises on her face that the babysitter could not explain. We began to brawl and the police were involved. After statements were taken, I rushed my daughter to the hospital for an examination. Thank God, there were no permanent damages to her other than a few bruises, and my broken heart. Needless to say, I took off the very next day to search for another babysitter. In those days there was no daycare that accommodated military working hours, so I had to go with a babysitter who worked from home. After I reported to work, I was ordered to report to my commander for disciplinary actions. It's a violation for soldiers to participate in any altercation. When I reported, my commander had the police report on his desk and was prepared to discipline me until I showed him the photos of my daughter's bruises that were taken at the hospital. Again, the angels were on my side, because he let me go with a warning. Unfortunately, I had a series of undesirable babysitters and I found myself cycling through babysitters like a race in a marathon. I couldn't wait for the time that she was old enough where she no longer needed a babysitter.

It was nearing time for me to complete my tour in Germany. In order to get a passport for my daughter, I needed to submit a copy of my birth certificate. I contacted my mom to have her send me a copy of my birth certificate. When I received the birth certificate I knew my mother had to have sent me the wrong one or someone else's. My name was nowhere on that birth certificate and even my mother's name was not familiar to me. Was I adopted? I do look different from my siblings. If I didn't look just like my mother, I would have sworn I was adopted. So why, then, was there a different name on the birth certificate? When I submitted the birth certificate to apply for my daughter's passport, it was declined, no surprise there. The Army refused to give my daughter a passport and I was told I would have to leave Germany without her. Neither the Army, Air Force, Navy, nor the Marines could force me on that plane without my daughter. They asked me to get a copy of my mother's birth certificate to match the name on my birth certificate. Unfortunately, it was written in Spanish and the military could not translate it. Again I was told I would have to leave my daughter in Germany. I contacted my mother and explained my situation and to ask her about my birth certificate. She explained that when I was born, she wrote the Spanish version of my first name and gave me my grandmother's last name because she was an illegal alien and in fear of deportation back to her country. She didn't want Immigration to find her and deport us back to the Dominican Republic. That's ironic because after she met my brother's dad, that's exactly what ended up happening. My mother, my brother, and I were deported to Dominican Republic when I was two years old and my brother was just a few months old. And my current last name that I knew all my life…well I got that from my brother's father who was supposed to legally adopt me but never had the chance. I was baptized when I was four years old and he was listed on the baptism certificate as my father and that is how I grew up with a different name on my birth certificate. I solicited the help of a military lawyer and explained my situation. I was made to give a sworn statement that I have lived all my life under my current name and I was given a passport for my daughter. That was it!

Years passed and I survived two divorces, two rape attempts, and sexual harassment by my superior. Twenty-one years after joining the military I retired with honorable service, an Associate's Degree, a Bachelor Degree, and a Master's Degree.

But it wasn't until I was 40 years old that my mom finally told me why she signed me up in the military. My mother had a plan to escape living in an abusive relationship. Her live-in boyfriend repeatedly beat her. My siblings and I watched helplessly when he would drag her on the ground, push her around, and beat her to a pulp. The only way she could escape was only after she knew that her kids were out of the house and were safe. So she enrolled me in the Army, my brother moved in with his pregnant girlfriend, and she packed whatever she could with my little sister and just left. She left behind furniture, a piano, our baby pictures, and everything else that would not fit in one little suitcase.

I am spiritually grateful for all the blessings bestowed on me and I know now that I have also inherited my strength from my mother. And my daughter? Well, my baby girl is now 30 years old with a successful career in journalism.

After life in the military, I travelled a new path into entrepreneurship. I became a real estate investor where I help low-income families live in affordable apartments. And after having a few health challenges just a few years ago, and educating myself on using food to heal, I became a Certified Health Coach in the Atlanta, Georgia, area. I help women realize that health changes don't have to change their lives.

Life continues to offer me new challenges, but I always remember that "this too shall pass." Life has a way of testing people's will, either by having nothing happen at all, or by having everything happen at once. The lessons I learned helped me to become better, stronger, and to leap into my destiny by upgrading my thinking and expanding my capacity.

ABOUT
LaWana Firyali Richmond, Ed.D

Dr. LaWana 'Firyali' Richmond serves as Staff Advisor to the Regents of the University of California and Senior Business Analyst at UC San Diego where her focus is project management and process improvement. Her background and experience are an eclectic mix of operations, technology, leadership, and social justice.

She is a certified Project Management Professional with degrees in Marketing, Operations, Information Systems, and Educational Leadership. She is one of the inaugural Chrispeels Fellowship recipients and completed the Joint Doctorate Program in Educational Leadership from UC San Diego and CSU San Marcos.

Her dissertation, "Black Staff Engagement at a Major Research University in Relation to Strategic Planning, Innovation, and Collaboration" was her way of converging topics of particular interest to her.

Dr. Richmond has also serves on the Advisory Board for the C. Montgomery Technology Fund, which supports community access to technology at the Malcolm X Library in southeast San Diego. An avid Toastmaster, she has chartered one club, sponsored another and served as an area governor. She is always enthusiastic about helping organizations move towards greater efficiency, effectiveness, and harmony.

Twitter:	@firyali @firyedu
Linkedin:	https://www.linkedin.com/in/lawanarichmond
Blogger:	http://livininmyhead.blogspot.com
Website:	www.firyali.com
Email:	info@firyali.com

DEFIANT SLACKER TO ALTRUISTIC HACKER

by LaWana Firyali Richmond, Ed.D

Throughout my life, I have had to apply ingenuity to develop innovative solutions with limited resources to leverage. I titled this piece from Defiant Slacker to Altruistic Hacker because of this. I'm using the definition of hacking that says: Hacking might be characterized as an appropriate application of ingenuity'.

When I was a young girl, I got distracted. I let my circumstances dictate my path. Instead of embracing the things that I now know make me special, I tried to "fit in." I wanted to be accepted by my perceived peers. I wanted to be accepted by the cool kids. Possibly because they were so different from most things that I am. Even in the midst of wanting to be cool, I was a math and science nerd. I was frequently called an L7 and my big dream was to go to MIT.

Meanwhile, the adults around me interpreted my behavior outside of the classroom to mean I was not living to my potential. They made choices about me and my education that didn't align with my goals. I dropped out of high school as an act of defiance when I felt that the grownups didn't understand me and didn't respect the path I had chosen. Yeah, I showed them. I even topped it off by having a baby when I was 16.

I remember the look of disappointment or disgust on the faces of people watching a 16-year old push a baby stroller. Some even went so far as to tell me how I had ruined my life. They told me I used to have a future but I had messed it off being silly. The words they used were actually less kind. I was told I would never amount to anything and that my child would never become anything either.

I remember bawling my eyes out when it all finally hit me. I was in my apartment with my baby and freshly aware of how clueless I was. I was a poor, uneducated, single, black, teenage mom. I had taken parenting classes, but they hadn't prepared me for the economic realities that I faced.

So I prayed. I asked the Creator to open my ears and guide my steps towards purpose. Although I struggled with issues associated with poverty for many years, I believe I have benefitted from nudges whenever I got too far off track.

I decided to take one step at a time towards something different and trust that it would work out. Even though I didn't become a saint, I began to take steps on faith. I started working at a donut shop as an Assistant Manager because some random person asked me if I wanted a job. I learned I liked to work. While working at a neighborhood record store, I had the experience of having a young college student walk in and become my boss. I didn't really understand quite how it worked but I knew from that point on that I needed to get an education.

I had no idea how or where to start. One day, I was at the mall and someone asked if I would be willing to respond to a brief survey. That survey led to me signing up for a trade school to get a certificate in bookkeeping. While there, I discovered that I loved school and particularly enjoyed human dynamics. But I chose bookkeeping because it seemed like a sure fire way to stay gainfully employed.

The business school I was attending ended up going out of business. I wasn't sure what to do, so I decided to get a GED and then went to an adult continuing education center to get some help figuring out what to do next. I completed a battery of tests that told me I had potential in a few different areas, but I chose to focus in on business competencies. I reasoned that I would be able to support my child with jobs in that area.

Even though I had taken courses at the business college and then completed my GED I decided to take a series of tests to validate my decision to pursue further education. I was filled with fear and anxiety as I walked onto the community college campus. I didn't know where to go or even what I was looking for. I just wandered around reading signs until I found something that looked like a main office.

Eventually, I enrolled and found my home at San Diego City College. The campus was small enough to be traversed in under 10 minutes and the coziness was mirrored in the class sizes and access to faculty. While there, I discovered an interest in student organizations and community activism. I explored my interests in the arts and humanities. I met my first mentor at that campus. To this day, when she and I cross paths we greet one another with a warm hug and words of encouragement. She taught me about love and acceptance of self and others. She taught me the power of self-love. She taught me how to give and receive love on both the micro and macro levels. She set me on the path of getting to know myself.

Even though I was consistently working towards self-sufficiency through education, I desperately wanted to get off of public assistance and provide for my child. Eventually, that desperation won and I took a break from college to work full time. For a while, my life consisted of going to work, trying to be a mom and acting my age. I was 20 and 21 at the time. One thing of note that happened during this period was doing some volunteer work with my mother for one of her friends. Her friend's husband was on the city council, so when the mayor's office was recruiting volunteers to support their resume building booth at the African American Women on Tour Conference, he turned to his wife. She turned to her friends, and my mother being a good friend, roped me in.

I'm so glad she did. I had never been around so many professional women. And had never seen so many black women in one place at one time. This was my introduction to how rewarding and developmental volunteer work can be. I was amazed by the style and confidence of the attendees. I was also blown away by the range of professions, industries, and enterprises they represented. I managed to get a small book of poetry into the hands of the one and only Susan L. Taylor that day. There was something that she said during her keynote speech which stuck with me. She encouraged all women to have economic independence. She shared an anecdote about the difference between nursing a broken heart while trying to figure out how to pay the bills and nursing a broken heart while nursing a fruity beverage in the Bahamas.

I gave birth to a second child. It soon became evident that I would have to be the sole provider for two children and the type of work available to me as an uneducated woman with minimal experience was not going to support a family. So back to school I went.

This time, I had to manage classes, work, and parenting two children. One in primary school and the other still in diapers. I believe this is where I first began to develop my skills as a project manager. I worked as an independent contractor supporting community organizations and small businesses through sales and marketing for their special events. Even this was the result of a mini faith walk. I saw a flier for a large and lovely beauty pageant. It piqued my interest after having failed to lose all the baby weight again. I thought it might be good for my self-esteem. When I got there, I found out the contestants had to pay fees. I liked the energy of the program, but wasn't comfortable paying any fees. I asked the producer if she had any paid positions. She said I could sell advertising and exhibit space. I didn't know what I was doing, but I quickly gained a degree of mastery. By the time the pageant happened, I was recruited to help another producer with their event. Eventually, my client base grew through word of mouth.

After many stops and starts, I petitioned for graduation from the community college only after my EOP counselor told me it was time to move on. I had so many units it was starting to not make sense for me to be there. I applied for and was admitted to San Diego State University's College of Business Administration.

By this point, I was on a mission. I worked, went to school and took my children everywhere while I engaged in community service. I served actively in student organizations and began to develop skills as a facilitator and presenter. Once again, I got distracted. I didn't graduate when I thought I was supposed to because I had one incomplete and had allowed my GPA to drop from 3.6 to under 2.0. That was the trade-off for working full time while going to school full time. Rather than jump right in and take care of it, I let that GPA and incomplete courses to hang over me for years.

The economy was better back then and I was busy working and getting married and being a wife. On top of everything else, I landed my dream job. I was working for African American Women on Tour. This was even better than being at the conference as a volunteer. I was being paid to do work I loved. The amount of passion and energy that I brought to making those conferences happen have been unsurpassed. The opportunity to provide content that was changing the lives of women all over the country was truly a blessing. Being exposed to high power executives and deep spiritual healers had an impact on me and my world view. I was able to appreciate my reflection in others and began to believe in infinite possibilities. My faith grew.

Throughout all of this, I was actively engaged in volunteering for community based organizations and educational institutions. Each of these things were and remain central to my psyche. My next job was working for the San Diego Urban League where I was responsible for helping to open 10 technology centers with access to computers and training for people in underserved communities as part of a federal workforce readiness grant. The work was rewarding and challenging. This was the first time my avocation and vocation were in alignment. Aside from some issues with internal personnel, I was happy there and I met one my best friends in life while working there. More than a friend, she is my sister to this day. I grew as a speaker and organizer and developed more start up acumen.

Then my marriage fell apart. After my divorce, I experienced some significant lifestyle changes. The economy took a big dip and I had a hard time finding gainful employment. I started a new job at a considerably lower salary. Eventually, I was motivated to go take care of my education situation because the economy had changed and competition was stiff.

When I was wrapping up my Bachelor of Science in Business Administration by taking courses at National University, my then boyfriend encouraged me to go on and do the Master's program while I was still in school mode. So I did. By 2005, just shy of twenty years after I was supposed to graduate from high school, I had a graduate degree in information systems.

For the past eleven years I have worked as an analyst in Business and Financial Services at UC San Diego, and institution recognized for its spirit of innovation and contributions to engineering and medicine. Quite often, I leverage creativity and critical thinking skills developed through years of having to find ways to make something out of nothing. Rather than being sad for my journey, I remind myself often that it prepared me to be uniquely qualified to approach innovation and problem solving in a different way

Recently, I completed a joint doctorate program in educational leadership offered by UC San Diego and CSU San Marcos and I was appointed to serve a two year term as Staff Advisor to the Regents where I travel throughout the state meeting with staff and leadership in support of communication, transparency, and employee engagement. I don't believe my journey is over, but I am comfortable with the idea that I have already accomplished far more than the sixteen year-old me imagined the day I realized how clueless I was.

ABOUT
Valerie M. Williams

Valerie is an emerging inspirational and motivational speaker that shares her message of faith and empowerment with everyone she meets. Williams is strategically and aggressively growing her own business as a Travel Professional and Co-Founder of V.A.L. Enterpryzes.

She plans to retire in the not so distant future from her day job as a is an Administrative Services Assistant for the State of Tennessee to enjoy a life of writing short stories, traveling as a public speaker and vacationing with family and friends.

Currently, Valerie attends Bethel World Outreach Church serving on the Prayer Team and for past 12 years she has dedicated her life to Christ as a Born Again Believer. She enjoys performing arts, singing, praising, praying, helping and encouraging others.

Fourteen years ago this single mother relocated from New York after 911, first moving to Georgia, then to Tennessee and she has not looked back. She is the proud mother of two adult children.

travel.valenterpryzes.com
marketing.valenterpryzes.com
tickets.valenterpryzes.com
valenterpryzes@yahoo.com

FAITH

By Valerie Williams-Torres

My name is Valerie; and I am no stranger to struggle. Looking back at my path – a path littered with diversity, challenge, love and change. I always look to God who is the author and finisher of my faith. Now the Bible says that faith is the substance of things hoped for and the evidence of things unseen. I am the proof of this concept and this is my story of how my faith carried me through some trying times in my life.

I remember once, early in my new focused – born again walk with God I went up to the alter for prayer and the pastor started praying for me and then all of a sudden as she was praying, she broke out into an intensified "cutting" session on me.

She began an all-out assault cutting me up (or what she saw) in the realm of the spirit. And as she was doing these frenzied cutting gestures with her hand that went from left to right, up and down, diagonally and here and there – I felt whipped! Then after about two minutes, she stepped back (still praying) she never stopped praying, she began looking far beyond me and politely walked back up to me for another two minute round of that all over again!

At that point she asked the clergy to hold me up and I'm sure what she was after or what was there, was surely dead and there no more by the time she got through. I didn't have a clue what was happening but I trusted her. Before I fell to the ground in a heap, she explained to me what she just did needed to be done for where I was going and for what I was going to go through and because of where I'd been.

Wow! I was no good in that moment. In that space of time I had been reduced to mush. But I believed it was for the glory of God and therefore, I was somewhat ok with it. In the scripture a prophet ate poop. A donkey talked. Another prophet was told to marry a prostitute. Abraham was asked to sacrifice his son. I mean I could go on and on. So maybe this was my little tidbit. All I knew is that I was seriously messed up on a multitude of levels after that whippin'.

There I lay in a fricasseed pile on the floor thinking – OMG! And I really didn't have the courage to ask God what that was really all about because honestly, in that moment I didn't want to know. To tell you the truth, I was shaking in my boots. So with a complete lack of understanding but with genuine sincerity I began to thank and praise God from somewhere real deep inside of me. Then I asked Him to strengthen me for what lies ahead because I knew and understood that He was Lord over my life and he said He'd never leave me nor forsake me. So - I said to myself, "God, I'm trusting you. I'm availing myself to you right now. You said you use the foolish to confound the wise."

Now, fast forward many years later and many faith walks later and I'm in the store doing some quick grocery shopping when my phone rings. I barely hear it because as usual it's buried deep inside my purse. I find it and see that it is one of my sisters, Von, and as I joyfully answered I was not expecting to hear what I couldn't stop or avoid. I remember wanting to go back to the previous day, the previous moment even the previous year – anything that would get me away from this. But there was no escape, no retreat only to go on through.

My sister was saying our perfect number of seven had been broken and that we weren't a complete set anymore. Now I'm in a grocery store trying to work my budget for dinner and I'm thinking to myself – what? What are you talking about woman? And then she said his name. I felt like someone was choking and stabbing me as she simply said "Jack" and I said, "Jack what?" And she said he's gone Val. I said, "Gone where?" And she said absolutely nothing. Nothing! Silence is all I heard and I'm thinking, well!? I said "Hello? Are you there?" And she said, "Yes." I said, "What are you talking about?"

Now, you have to understand that my mom and dad together had eight children. Five girls and three boys with a set of fraternal twins in there. One of my sisters we never knew because according to my mom, she only lived a week and passed on. We knew about her because when we were little we had this mammoth sized bible that my mom read out of and showed us all the color pictures and in the front it had genealogy pages and stuff.

Her name was there listed with ours in the birth records but was listed by itself under recorded deaths. She was born a year after me and would have been between myself and my brother, Jack.

What my sister, Von, was trying to tell me as I stood there in the store is that we had lost a brother. She was telling me this about one of my younger and well-loved brothers.

I could see the front door of the store but was a good distance away from it, and knew I needed to make a b line for that door quick fast and in a hurry. As I tried to sort this all out and grasp what I was hearing - I in the dark on what she was really saying.

In deep denial, I was calm at first and very matter of fact as I told her it was a lie and that somebody was lying because God wouldn't let that happen to *my* brother. Adamantly I told her they made a mistake and insisted she go back and get the facts and get it right.

All that disappeared as I cracked under what she said next. She said my mom's baby sister, my Aunt Delores, had already been to the morgue and identified him. So then I got mad and said auntie didn't know what she was talking about and somebody else needed to go down there and prove that it isn't our brother.

I guess God had to slap me. My sister then let me know that she sent me the pictures auntie had taken of him when she went to ID him, and that I should look at my phone because it was him. She said she looked at the pictures already and it is him. By then I was running and screaming and I wasn't even near the door. It was a blood curdling scream of anguish. I collapsed outside and dropped to the ground yelling at God insisting that He bring my brother back right now because I knew He was capable of doing it. Of course that didn't happen and I had to come to the realization that I'd lost a sibling.

You know, some years earlier this same brother had lost one of his sons, Rodney. I remember him asking me if I would get up and speak at the service. Thinking about that, I knew I had to speak at my brother's service because he wouldn't have it any other way.

Do you think this is what my pastor saw when she was cutting me in the spirit that day? I don't know but I am grateful for my faith, for God, for restoration and for healing. Being grateful carries a lot of weight. No, not the kind of weight that comes from carrying a heavy and laborious load. But the weight of the full and total goodness of God through the humility of recognition.

To recognize where you are as opposed to where you were. Today my life gives credibility to the words in the phrase that speaks to folks having come a "mighty long way". Success speaks volumes and says many different things to different people. It varies and ranges from the miniscule to the colossal; and stems from the inner knowing of having accomplished and attained. Having stepped out and having withstood and emerged New! Victorious! Shatter Proof! A Bed Rocked Warrior reflecting a soldier's stance.

Having come through all of this to get to the other side, I often what to shout, Hallelujah! Hallelujah all the day long – like a song unsung in the hearts of the less fortunate that became fortunate. Like the least likely to succeed, who escaped and or broke through – succeeded – got free and continued to break through barriers that sought to stifle, stop and limit. All because of Faith!

ABOUT
Jeselle L. Eli, MPH

Renowned success coach, international speaker and author Jeselle Eli, is one of the top trailblazers in the coaching and self-help field. After being diagnosed with a life-threatening disease at the age of 22, Jeselle thought her life was over, but it was just the beginning. She embarked on a transformational journey that helped her create a life that surpassed her wildest dreams.

Jeselle has been a special guest on radio and television programs around the country. She is using her powerful story of tragedy and triumph to enhance the lives of millions around the world. While a student, Jeselle produced and hosted her own radio show, titled "Let's Talk About It" with Jeselle on WRBB, which featured interviews with celebrities.

Her clients include Planned Parenthood and the Elton John AIDS Foundation. Jeselle holds a Bachelor's of Science degree in Communications from Northeastern University in Boston, a Master's in Public Health from Monroe College and is a Certified NLP Practitioner.

Email: Jeselle@JeselleEli.com
Tel: (646) 535-8232
Website: www.JeselleEli.com

SOCIAL MEDIA PAGES

Facebook: JeselleEli
Twitter   justjeselle
LinkedIn: https://www.linkedin.com/in/JeselleEli
YouTube: https://www.youtube.com/user/JeselleTV
Instagram: JeselleEli

LIFE DOESN'T HAPPEN TO YOU, IT HAPPENS FOR YOU

by Jeselle L. Eli, MPH

Imagine, it was my junior year of college and I was pursuing a dream when everything came crashing down in an instant. At the time, being a radio and television host was the only thing on my mind. I already had four years under my belt of hosting my own show at my college station, Northeastern's WRBB. It was the best part of my day. I didn't care what time I had to wake up, as long as I could play the music, get behind the microphone, and share the news with the listeners everything was alright by me. However, for a few months of my junior year I had a secret dark side going on during my spare time. You see, one day I was introduced to crack and I tried it. The man who lived upstairs used to go and buy weed for me and one day he left me with a little baggie filled with this rock. I didn't know what it was. He just told me to watch it for him. I had taken a little piece of it thinking when I figured out what to do with this, I will give it a try. However, when he came back from getting my bag of weed, he offered some of this new drug to me. He showed me how to set it up and that's how it all began. One pull. I honestly didn't even know if I was high. I had to think a lot about it and wondered what just happened. Which immediately made me want to take another pull to help me understand what was going on. Then I started doing things like looking at myself in the mirror and watching my eyes dilate. That would amuse me for whatever reason. The strange drug curbed my appetite and I thought I could continue to use it on occasion just to lose weight. What started out as a little curiosity became a habit that grew into an addiction which morphed into a group activity that quickly became dangerous.

My apartment became a haven for my secret addiction. It was never a forced indulgence. It was just my stupid and naïve curiosity for drugs that lead me to it. Each day after I left school, I would call my dealer to get my purchase ready for my arrival home. After a while I eventually invited the other users from upstairs into my apartment and that's when things got ugly. We would binge for days and this eventually led to some risky sexual behavior. When we ran out of the drug, I would crawl on the floor and try and find more in the carpet. Even on the street, my head was always looking down thinking I could find a little piece somewhere. I completely missed the beauty of the neighborhood because I was living in an apartment off campus. Nobody really knew what was going on in my secret world.

When a few friends came over and saw the state of my place I'm sure they thought something was up because that was unusual for it to be such a pigsty. My parents started to know something was not right when I started asking for hundreds of dollars by the week. I used to lie and say that I was using it for school projects. One day they just showed up at my door and I had to hide everything. But when they came in and saw the state of the place, then never sent another dime.

I have always been the experimental and adventurous type, but this was the lowest point I have ever taken myself. I don't know what came over me. But one thing I do know for sure is that once you put that pipe to your mouth the devil enters your body and only God can save you. And I truly believe that He saved me. I remember the day so clearly that the people from upstairs invited me to their apartment. They had alcohol, crack, and cocaine spread out everywhere. They had a bed laid out on the floor. They had lingerie in my size. In my mind I was excited, I was ready to party. But something came over me, a higher power that I had no control of. This power, I chose to believe it was God, walked me out the door and back to my apartment. I immediately packed a bag and went to the bus station. I took a bus from Boston to New York and I went straight to the hospital for help. I remember getting off the bus at Penn Station and walking to a pay phone at the corner of 8th Ave and 42nd street. I called 911 and said, "Please help me." A few minutes later an ambulance rolled up and took me to the hospital. That night could have been my last night if God did not intervene.

Because I was now in the hospital, the drug use came to a screeching halt. I was there for about six weeks. When I came out I did have to take a little time to get my mind back together. Once I recovered, I took a little break from classes at Northeastern. However, I did decide to complete an internship for school. During that time one bit of news changed my life forever. I did part of my internship in Atlanta, GA, and before I left I went to all of my doctors to update my visits. While away, I got calls from my gynecologist repeatedly to come in to follow up with my exam. I put it off because I was so far away from NY. Three months later, I went home to NY and saw my OB/GYN. The exact words that came out of her mouth were, "Jeselle, all of your tests came back fine except for one test. Your HIV test came back positive." I looked at her and my insides went numb. I pulled my hands to my face and started crying. This was the last thing I could be expecting to hear at 23 years old. She came to me with a tissue in one of her hands, she put the other one on my back and said, "God doesn't do anything to you that you can't handle." I won't tell you what I said back to her! But I was furious.

She helped me navigate telling another health professional in my life and telling my mother. I immediately told a friend. And then I had to go home and face my father. That's a whole other story, with strict Caribbean parents you can only imagine how tough this next step was for me. My parents never knew the extent of my drug use, but they did know something was not right with me. Adding an HIV diagnosis was more news for them to manage at one time. Long story short, that night I went to bed. I felt like I went to sleep and never woke up again. I felt dead inside. I felt worthless, dirty, and ashamed. I also felt unlovable. The list could go on and on. It was hard to imagine this super vivacious, bubbly girl who all of a sudden went lifeless. But I did and I had to learn how to be this new me. A version of me that I didn't quite like. This is where the process of personal development played an enormous role in my life because I had to learn to love myself again. It was easy for me to share these same tools with other people as I learned to master them myself.

After my diagnosis, I immediately felt like my dreams were at a standstill. I went on to continue my last year of college. I still had my radio show but you could tell that something happened to me. My voice was not the same chipper-sounding voice it used to be. During my senior year, I began acting in a play called "That Takes Ovaries." That got me involved again with interacting with people in a way that I was missing due to my depressive hibernation state. The play was a compilation of stories of bold and brazen women. The format of the play consisted of having an open mic at the end where people could share their stories of bravery. My best friend who has been my rock during all of this decided that one day she was going to share my story at the end of the one of the performances. She went on stage and said that recently her best friend was diagnosed with HIV and had thought that her life was over, but she started doing things she loves again and she is so proud to her smiling and laughing again like I used to (Note: I'm not sure what the author means here). I was shedding tears on the side of the stage and I decided to be bold and I got up gave her a hug and I turned to the audience and I said, "The woman that she is talking about is me." I then went on to share the rest of my story. In that moment I felt the weight of the world being lifted off of my shoulders. There was something so relieving about being vulnerable and transparent. It was then that I realized that sharing my story could possibly inspire someone else who may have been going through a hard time.

So I went home, soaked in the tub with a glass of wine, and pondered on this new calling. The writer of the play asked me to share my story at every open mic and I did. I also began doing workshops with at-risk groups as a result of this experience. Once I graduated, I moved to Brooklyn and started volunteering my time with organizations like Planned Parenthood, NYU, and Project Streetbeat to do HIV outreach in the communities. From different events I met many people and was then able to book myself as a speaker and HIV educator at schools and churches in Harlem, Brooklyn, and Manhattan. My speaking engagements started to take place nationally at universities in the U.S. and even internationally at schools and organizations. While I was working in real estate, I attended my first Tony Robbins event. That was a game changer for me and shortly afterwards I decided to train to become a life coach. I started coaching people and helping them bring their lives to the next level. I was building my business on the side while working. I still never let go of the dream of working in radio or television and in 2011 I got hired at A&E Television Networks. I felt like I what I went to school for finally paid off. The work that I was doing to teach people about HIV education and prevention had become such a passionate part of my life. I realized that my purpose in life had changed. An opportunity came up for me to go to Zambia, Africa, to intern for a year with an organization called Grassroot Soccer. Grassroot Soccer used the power of soccer to educate youth about HIV. It was an amazing program that reaches hundreds of thousands of youths and people in the communities in many countries around Africa. I was super excited to live abroad and give back to the community. I left my job and went into this unsure of where it would leave me once it was over, but I knew I had to reach more people. Working with youth in Africa was one of the most rewarding experiences I have ever had in my life. When I returned from my time abroad I decided to pursue my Masters in Public Health and I am now working at a hospital as Program Coordinator of Sexual Health Prevention Services.

When I was a teenager, I always thought that by the time I turned 25 I would have everything all figured out and that I would be on the straight path to success. The reality is that success is no straight path at all. It is a curvy road of ups and downs. And it takes a hell of a lot of resilience to travel. Now that I am turning 35, when I look back, I realize that my GYN was right in saying "God doesn't give you anything that you can't handle." I say that because I took something that I could have become the worst possible situation in my life and I turned it around. I took care of myself and in the process I helped others. I furthered my education. I stepped out beyond my own backyard. I got my sense of adventure back. I set a new standard for my life. Plus, I made really great friends along the way. And all of this was against the odds, because that very first day of hearing my diagnosis, I thought it was all over for me and that nothing good could ever possibly happen again but that wasn't my truth.

Tony Robbins put it best when he says "life doesn't happen to you, it happens for you." Therefore it is important to embrace what is happening or has happened in your life. Reevaluate what you can do to turn around that story or situation to make it work in your favor. Let your life support you. Don't let it bring you down. We all have those spaces that need a light shined on it from time to time to make us realize that we are not alone and that everyone is going through something. Find your support system. Find the people in your corner. Step into your power, step into your authentic true self. Your spirit will do wonders for the next soul who is yearning for your message. It's not worth it to look back a say I wish, I woulda, or coulda. Remember that you are not alone in your dark place and you can turn around anything you put your mind to. Take it from me because my tragedy has turned into my career and I am loving it.

ABOUT
Julia D Shaw

Julia D. Shaw is the Lead Consultant at Shaw Biz Consulting (SBC) formerly Shaw Literary Group. SBC provides traditional and non-traditional consultation services supporting business growth and development. Shaw's insight has proven beneficial to entrepreneurs, small businesses, publishers, authors, corporations, radio stations, educational institutions and non-profit organizations.

Shaw's professional experience spans over twenty years. Her latest business venture is a publishing partnership with Toni Coleman Brown compiling *Delayed But Not Denied: 20 Stories About Life and Resiliency.* Julia consults with the Network Journal Magazine's -40 Under Forty Achievement Awards and the 25 Influential Women in Business Awards.

Shaw and/or her clients have been featured in the NY Amsterdam News, NY Daily News, NY Times, USA Today, the Network Journal Magazine, Black Enterprise Magazine among a host of newspapers, blogs/websites, TV and radio shows

Shaw is a contributing author to the Amazon Bestseller, *Network to Increase Your Net Worth*, compiled by Toni Coleman Brown and was featured in *Steppin' Out with Attitude: Sister, Sell your Dream*, by Anita Bunkley. Julia is the proud mother of two daughters with three grandchildren, residing in Queens, NY.

Website:	shawbizconsulting@gmail.com www.shawbizconsulting.com www.delayedbutnotdenied.info
LinkedIn:	julia_d_shaw1
Facebook:	juliadshaw1 meettheauthorexperience
Twitter:	@juliadshaw1
Linkedin:	juliadshaw

IT'S NEVER TOO LATE TO BE A FATHER TO YOUR CHILDREN

By Julia D. Shaw

My oldest daughter was pregnant with her second child! Thirteen years after giving birth to my #1 grandson. He is my only grandson so I can say #1 in all fairness. She always wanted more than one child. It was two months before the delivery of the baby and everyone's excited! A team of her friends planned the baby shower and all I had to do was show up to support my baby girl. I was loving it. Then she dropped the bomb one day and said, "My dad is coming to my baby shower."

I immediately got very angry! She knew it would upset me and that's why she gave me two months' notice in an effort to get my mind right before the big event. I was steaming mad! It was so unfair! As a single mother I did all the hard work without any assistance from him! No child support. No taking her for the weekend to give me a mommy break. No taking her school shopping. In fact, the only graduation where he wasn't in jail was when she graduated with her Master of Science degree in Literacy. She is a teacher. So, yes, I was tight! It wasn't fair that he gets to pop back up and be a part of the family celebrations. I did all the work and he could just show up and be Super Dad and receive all the glory. Tears are falling as I write this piece because letting go and forgiving for me is an ongoing process. But now that she is an adult, she has decided to have him in her life. And yet again, I had to be the bigger person. I just couldn't understand why do I have to be the bigger person all the time?!

So I had to "play nice in the sandbox" whether I wanted to or not. My grown daughter wanted her father to be at this celebration of life and I had to accept that because there was nothing I could do about it. At that time I was living in my daughter's home and to add insult to injury, he was going to be staying at her house while he was visiting from Florida.

The baby shower was awesome! Her team of lifelong friends all dressed in white did an excellent job of planning and organizing this event. That weekend family and friends came in town from all over. My brother and his family came from Delaware; my second cousin, his wife, and daughter came in from Atlanta; my youngest daughter, who moved to California, surprised her and came home. My daughter's two half-sisters were also there. One of them came in all the way to New York from California.

See, my oldest daughter has two sisters in addition to the one I gave birth to and five half-brothers. They all know and love each other as brothers and sisters. Half or whole blood relations was never an issue. They all shared the same "rolling stone, not in their life as a child, father."

The baby shower was drama free, a true family celebration. The only drama was the inner turmoil that I was feeling with him being there, having a good time, enjoying the gift of just being in the presence of my beautiful daughter and her family. But she was happy! She even posted on Facebook about her father and future husband painting the baby's room a beautiful pink. Her comment was something like, "the two men in my life working together!" I tried my best to suffer quietly. But I wanted to yell at the top of my lungs, "Get the smile off your face! Get out of here! You did nothing to earn this experience of joy and celebration! Go back to where you came from! You are not welcome in my family's lives!" But the truth was, he was welcomed by his child and there was nothing I could do but accept it. There were a few situations that gave me flashbacks of my struggles as a single mother and the reasons why I made the hard decision to leave the father of my first daughter when she was a mere two years old.

Sometimes our children in their youthful wisdom can help us through our issues. His presence opened old wounds that in my mind I thought were healed. After he went back to Florida, I struggled with killing this anger dead and my daughter realized this when we would talk about him. During our conversation about the shower my words of unfairness surfaced again. She told me, "Mommy let it go! The fact is that I am 32 years old and there were people at the baby shower that I grew up with, many from childhood, high school, and my college years, not to mention people that I have met when I became an educator over 10 years ago and this was the first time that they have met my father. Even family that have known me all my life were not familiar with my father. These same people know you have always been there for me. They can see that he just came on the scene." This statement changed me. It was healing. These words were of great comfort coming from my daughter who loves her mother with all her heart. Although she is grown and is finally getting the opportunity to be "Daddy's Little Girl," she will never lose sight of the bond we share that stemmed from us being a team, without his help. Having a loving relationship with her father is all I ever wanted for her, for both of my daughters.

So, with every story there are multiple sides or storylines and from time to time I try to look at life from his current viewpoint. Now, that he is older and at times wiser, I can give him credit for being in the process of trying to be a better person. He has apologized to me many times in recent years for not being there. I don't remember the first couple of times he apologized, I heard the words but hearing them did not heal my heart or ease the pain that has plagued me for years. The words had no meaning, no cure of past ills. I just kept beating him up with angry words, wanting him to feel my pain and the struggles of being abandoned by a man I thought loved me and my child. I believed him when he sold me the dream of being a family. Sorry could not ease the pain nor heal my broken heart. I have to respect that regardless of my reaction, he continues in his own, sometimes crazy way to close the decades' worth of old open wounds that have not healed yet while I still fester with resentment towards him. He has complimented me an enormous amount of times on what a wonderful job I did raising our daughter and he always thanked me for that. He is grateful, as he says, "to just be in the room." Indicating that he realizes some of his mistakes and the impact they have had on the quality of the lives of others, mainly his children and the mothers who have raised them alone in his absence. While I am angry for him not being there for my daughter, he has seven other children that were missing his presence in their lives as well. Nonetheless, his words are the beginning to making amends to his past and secondly, his presence means a lot to his three daughters who are all grown.

When my daughter got married and had the wedding of her dreams, part of that dream was to have her father walk her down the aisle. This made my daughter very happy and that's all any mother wants for their child, happiness!

I noticed that for some reason the daughters are more forgiving of their dad being absent from their childhood. My daughters' five brothers, on the other hand, were not as forgiving. They are now men that challenge their father as a man. They do not overlook any shortcoming is his process of growth to be a better father. To my knowledge, they just have not gotten over the impact of being "fatherless sons."

I understand the pain and regret he is going through as a man who missed out on milestones in the lives of his children. Coming to terms and working hard to move forward to be the best possible father to his grown children that he can be has to be acknowledged for a moment in time.

My youngest daughter's father and ex-husband (yes, I married him thinking things would be different) was missing in action as a Dad too. There is six-year age difference between by daughters. I thought he was different. I thought he was a better man, better father, because he was a law enforcement officer. In retrospect, hindsight being 20/20, we should have never gotten married. Neither of us was ready for commitment and we got married for all the wrong reasons. While we were married I gave birth to another precious daughter whom I didn't realize wouldn't have her father in her life as a child. When this became my reality I realized there was nothing I could do, but be the best single mom I could possibly be in spite of all my issues of anger and unfairness.

They have come to terms with the past and are working towards a father-daughter relationship and all I can do is pray that it works out. She too is "Daddy's Little Girl." Although she is grown, a mother, and a sailor in the United States Navy, having her father in her life as a woman gives her the kind of support and love that she needs now. It builds a sense of confidence that a mother cannot provide.

At some point it crossed my mind that I was a statistic. Accepting the reality that I am a single black woman raising her children by herself was difficult, to say the least. The reality hit me hard. I remember that moment, I cried and cried, I never wanted to be in the category of a single black woman raising children by herself, but that was my reality. To move forward in my life I had to overcome the pain that pulled on my heartstrings. This pain controlled me and so many aspects of my life. I knew at some point I had to let go and allow greater things to happen in my life. My daughters have, and now it is my turn. It was a process that didn't happen overnight.

Two thoughts helped pull me through my unwanted reality. One was that the only person that feels my anger is me and being angry all the time wasn't going to change my level of responsibility and make our lives better. Ok, it wasn't fair, now what? Keep it moving! Get your life together! The second thought that kept me going was that they (the absentee fathers) were missing out on two beautiful young ladies growing up and it was their loss. One day they would realize the once-in-a-lifetime experiences they missed, like the first day of school, graduations, birthdays, dance school recitals. I was blessed to be a part of all that.

The financial struggles were real and over the years times were tough. My faith in God, my faith in myself, and the support of my family and friends pulled me through. "It takes a village to raise a child" and I can truly thank God for the support so many people gave me over the years. Some of the support was financial, but what I valued most from my friends and family was the moral support. Their life experience of raising their children and being on the outside looking in just long enough to give me great feedback. This all helped me with my parenting style and skills.

I know several other men who were not hands-on fathers while their kids were young, but are very present in the lives of their adult children and in my mind that is a wonderful thing. The healing process has to begin somewhere for the dysfunctional family dynamics of single parenthood, especially in communities of people of color. Love, understanding, and respect must prevail in the family unit throughout the world.

Part of my life's purpose is to help as many parents as I can through the process of dealing with the ups and downs of single parenthood, especially single moms with teenage daughters. If sharing experiences can help one mom work through the daily emotions and drama that comes with parenting, then I have made a difference. And to think, all I ever wanted for my girls was to have their fathers in their lives and here I was being mad when I was getting exactly what I had wanted. Their relationships with their dads were delayed, but they were not denied.

ABOUT
Lucrece Augusma

A native of Port-au-Prince, Haiti, Lucrece Augusma, is an entrepreneur, bestselling author, and educator. She is the CEO of Envisi8 Solutions, a business consulting and event planning firm helping individuals bring their vision to reality. She is also the Vice-Chairperson on the Worshipers' House of Prayer Academy Board.

Email:	alucrece.whopa@gmail.com
Facebook:	lucrece.augusma
Twitter:	GreatnessMay7
LinkedIn:	envisi8

FROM DELAY TO TRIUMPH

By Lucrece Augusma

I could remember this time in my life like yesterday. It was the summer of 2011 and my mother and I sat face to face in our living room. I remember the hurt in my Mother's voice when she told me that we could no longer afford to live in our apartment. I responded, "Okay, cool. All we have to do is look for another apartment." She sat there quietly, avoiding my eyes.

"What's wrong, Mom?" I asked.

"I am afraid that it won't be that easy," she reluctantly said.

"What do you mean?" I asked.

She went on to tell me that she was approved for senior housing and that I would have to live on my own. At that time, living on my own was not feasible due to my financial circumstances. My debts disproportionately exceeded my income. On top of that I had no savings. I also had no car and I was dependent on public transportation. That was a dark day for me, but it was also a big turning point in my life. One that shifted from me to a place of comfort, which I had living with my mom, to a place of desperation and near depression.

I searched all over for housing options that fit my situation. I even asked church friends, Facebook friends, and even some strangers for help, to no avail. So I was faced with the inevitable, which was homelessness. I couldn't believe that I was actually homeless. I ended up living at my church for one whole year. Imagine people silently pitying you and wishing they could help. Imagine asking for a ride somewhere and being told repeatedly, "I'm not going that way. Sorry." Sometimes I would have to walk miles to the purchase items I needed to take care of myself and earn money to pay off my debt. Imagine after service having to wait until everybody would leave to go home to set up my makeshift bed in the sanctuary so no one will know your situation. I had to endure this ordeal for ONE WHOLE YEAR!

I tell you that this experience was hard for me. It was so hard that I would cry every night asking and pleading with God to try to understand what I did wrong. I paid my tithes regularly. I tried to do everything right. I respected people. I helped people build their dreams. But what about me? I would say these things to myself over and over. But one day it hit me. I said enough is enough. I MUST rise above this situation because I knew that I was not destined for failure. I began to create a business plan for my brand, Envisi8. God sent encouraging people to push me such as my pastor and his family, some coworkers, and my mother. These individuals knew what I was going through and supported me. I began to change my mindset and the way I spent my money. I decided I was going to use this delay to better myself in every area of my life.

Lessons Learned

Through this dire situation I learned many important lessons that enabled me to turn my situation around. But there are 3 lessons that were a game changer for me. I believe that these lessons can also be a game changer for anyone who is going through a delay.

1. **Expect delays, but keep the right mindset.**
   When you are on the road to a certain destination, delays are inevitable. Whether it be a simple traffic jam or a flat tire. You must keep your cool and focus on where you are going. Getting upset with road rage or kicking your tires is not going to get you anywhere fast. The best solution would be to find a detour or get help with fixing that tire. I learned that I had to keep a good mindset even though I was in a hard place. I noticed that all of the "Why me" questions weren't getting me anywhere. I also noticed that getting upset and crying myself to sleep only kept me stuck in that traffic jam of poverty and lack. It wasn't until I changed my mindset that I discovered that there was a detour out of this mess. So a good mindset will transport you from setback to bounce back!

2. **Words are powerful, but actions are dynamite.**
   I remember the day I decided to change my mindset, I began to speak life to my dead situations. Every day I began to use Scriptures

and positive quotes to encourage myself and to stay focused on my goals of getting a car, getting a place to live, and starting to build my dream company. I didn't only stop there. It was only when I took action on what was spoken, that explosive change began to happen. That is why I believe that although words are powerful, actions are DYNAMITE! There are some situations you face in life that require more than just mere words. Don't just say what you want to happen, but MAKE IT HAPPEN! Your words need to be backed up by action to blow that setback or delay out of your life.

3. **Listen to your GPS.**

   Have you ever tried to create your own "shortcut" and ignored your GPS? Sometimes so called "shortcuts" can become big delays. God is our GPS, gently prompting us with step-by-step direction. We have to listen to what He tells us to do in order to fulfill our purpose. Trying to do it our own way will only lead to more delay and frustration. Staying connected through prayer and His Word will ensure you reach your destination of abundance.

From Delay to Triumph

I am a living testimony that delays do not last forever and that there is always a light at the end of the tunnel. Weeping may endure for a night, but joy (and all the other splendid benefits) comes in the morning. God has brought me from despair to encouraging other people. I came from a position of lack to a position of provision. Now I can provide for my family here and abroad. I came from having no car to driving a fully paid car. I came from being homeless to living in a place of my own, paying rent on time. I came from having dreams and goals written on paper to being the CEO of Envisi8 Solutions, a brand ready to change the world. I did all this through Christ who strengthens me. And guess what? YOU CAN TOO!

These changes didn't happen overnight. For me it seemed like a major delay. But I soon discovered that this delay was actually preparation for something greater. Do not despise delays and setbacks. Look them in the eye and tell them "I am bigger than you!" Be bold. Be courageous. Change your mindset. Change your world.

ABOUT

ABOUT
Toni Coleman Brown

Toni Coleman Brown is an author, coach, marketing expert and motivational speaker. She is also the CEO and Founder of the Network for Women in Business, an online community for women business owners who seek affordable cutting-edge training and the ability to connect and advance with other like-minded individuals. The motto for the Network is, "We EDUCATE to ELEVATE women in business." Toni is also the creator of the Small Business Bootcamp for Women and the Online Marketing Mastermind Live events.

Toni been featured in the NY Amsterdam News, the Network Journal Magazine, Our Time Newspaper Black Enterprise Online, Working Woman Magazine and WPIX 11's Working Woman Report. She is the author of *"Quantum Leap: How to Make a Quantum Leap in Your Network Marketing Business"* and the compiler and co-author of *"Network to Increase Your Net Worth"* and *"Delayed But Not Denied: 20 Stories of Life and Resiliency."*

Toni is on a mission to fulfill her God-ordained purpose of changing the lives of millions. Toni lives in Queens, New York with her husband and two daughters.

Email:	toni@networkforwomeninbusiness.com
Website:	www.networkforwomeninbusiness.com
	www.tonicolemanbrown.com
	www.smallbusinessbootcampforwomen.com
	www.onlinemarketingmastermindlive.com
Facebook:	tonicolemanbrown
Twitter:	@tonibrown
Instagram:	tonicolemanbrown

THE PAST DOES NOT EQUAL THE FUTURE

By Toni Coleman Brown

"No! No! No!" I screamed out. But the look on his face clearly showed that he didn't hear me. Nor did he care. He kept fighting me. Looking at him at that moment was like looking straight into the eyes of evil. I couldn't recall when he left his body and the devil took over. As the car swerved back and forth on Interstate 10, I yelled "Take Me Home! Take Me Home!" repeatedly. But he didn't listen. He continued to throw blows while he drove towards his house in a feeble attempt to allow me to get myself together before taking me home. This was the routine. He'd hit me and then take me to his house so I could get myself together before he'd take me back home to my parents' house. But this time I cried and I screamed, "Take Me Home!" And this time, I also fought him back. He lived near a graveyard and as we passed by I remember saying, "One of us is going to end up in this graveyard and I'm telling you right now that it's not going to be me!" When he finally made it to my parent's house, I jumped out of his car and vowed that I would never ride in it again.

It was a dreadful night. One that I would never forget. It was supposed to be perfect. It was the night of my high school graduation party. One that I had planned with a few of my classmates. But it was cut short because of jealously. It all started when my girlfriend asked me to come to the door of the clubhouse where we were having the party to see if she could get her boyfriend's male friend into the party. Somehow, he thought her boyfriend was trying to set me up with his friend. Not! But those erroneous thoughts caused the night to end with me running inside my childhood home seeking refuge with my family.

My hair was a mess, my clothes were disheveled, and blood stains were on my cream- colored blouse. My mom was the only one home at the time and when I arrived she looked at me confused. She couldn't understand what was going on. He had already pulled away from the driveway, so he wasn't available to answer any questions. But this was the night that I finally broke my silence and revealed to her that my high school boyfriend had been beating me. I was embarrassed and confused. But most of all, I was tired of living in fear and I was done with his abuse. Honestly, I couldn't understand how I had gotten to this place. However, this was not the same person with whom I fell massively in love during my freshman year.

Randy Rose was three years older than me. He had perfect caramel skin and a high afro. He wore glasses that made him look like he could have been the birth son of Arthur Ashe. He was about 6'2 with nice broad shoulders and a slim build. Oh, yeah, he was fine. He didn't come from a wealthy background, so he had a job and worked for everything he had and I admired that. When he got his first car it was an old, white Buick 66. He loved that car, but it was always breaking down. So he worked hard and purchased a brown '82 Camaro sports car. You couldn't tell him that he wasn't the man. I was proud of him. I was attracted to his fortitude. It seemed as if whatever he put his mind to, he was able to accomplish. This fit perfectly with my go-getter attitude and work ethic. College wasn't on his agenda, even though it was on mine. I was fine with the idea of him going into the service. We would meet up together at the end.

Everything was perfect between us for about three years. It wasn't until I ended my junior year that things began to go awry. I was so excited about going into the 12th grade, being a senior, and graduating. I entered that year full of hope. But it didn't turn out to be a good year at all. First, I found out too late that I couldn't go to Howard University because I had not taken the SATs. And second, things with way south with our relationship. I don't know if it was because he was afraid that I was going to pass him up or move on without him, but it seemed as if he became paranoid about everything. If I said hello to my male friends, who were also his friends, he started to have a problem. I was on the dance team and he all of a sudden had a problem with me doing that, so I quit to avoid any problems. And anyone who *really* knew me also knew that I loved to dance. But it's funny how no one even questioned me when I quit.

Life for me became odd. I became distant from my friends. Folks just characterized me as quiet. I just focused on him, work, and school. But as good and focused as I was, that wasn't good enough. I was a good girlfriend. I never cheated. Well, there was that one time I kissed someone from the band. But it was only after things had started to get so twisted in our relationship. There was just no explanation for the kind of crazy into which this dude morphed. So that night was the end of an era for me.

I honestly felt as if a 200lb. weight had been lifted off of me. But freedom didn't come easy. I spent the entire summer looking over my shoulder because letting go wasn't easy for Randy. One day, when I was leaving from my job at the bank, as I walked to my car, he popped out from behind a tree. I was terrified. I tried to rush to get in my car, but that didn't work. When he swung at me, I lifted up my arm to shield my face. After one hard punch that missed my face, but landed on my arm, I decided to run to get the security guard. By the time we got back to the car, he was nowhere in sight. The only thing that was left was a bruise the size of a baseball on my arm. I was just lucky that it wasn't on my face.

Later that summer, I met someone new. I was so happy to be free to see other people. One night when my new beau was leaving the house he said he saw someone outside. I immediately told him to come back inside and locked the door. It was Randy hiding along the side of the house. After this incident, my family had a conversation with his mother and explained what had been going and what the consequences would be if he didn't leave me alone. After that chat, I didn't see Randy again for years.

But I did hear about him. I heard that he was in another tumultuous relationship and that his new girlfriend had a baby. This news caused me to pause and think about the baby that I had gotten rid of. When I was 17 years old and in my junior year, I got pregnant. I begged my mother to allow me to have an abortion. She was dead against it. She told me that I was going to have that baby and that I was going to marry Randy and he would go into the service while I stayed home. When she said those words, I saw my life flash before my eyes. I knew I couldn't have a baby with this crazy person. But at that time my mom didn't know what was going on. I guess my begging worked because she took me to her OB-GYN and he confirmed the pregnancy and we made an appointment at another clinic and she took me there to have the procedure. It was all a blur. I can vaguely remember feeling crampy like I just had a bad period once it was all over.

I later learned that Randy named his baby girl Pherrin. I was taken aback because my favorite niece was named Ferron. I thought this was creepy. A few years later I found myself a sophomore at Howard University. Yes, I was delayed by one year, but I wasn't denied my dream of attending Howard. After one year of attending Dillard University in New Orleans, I transferred to HU. I remember one day hanging out with my roommates when I heard the news that Randy had murdered his girlfriend, who had become his wife. She had just delivered their second baby just six weeks prior. I heard that he stabbed her repeatedly and left her on the kitchen floor covered with a blanket. I heard he took the kids to his mom's house and fled the state. My roommates and I felt scared and nervous because we all believed that Randy was on his way to find me. But he turned himself over to the police in Atlanta. My roommates teased me and said they believed he was coming my way. Deep down inside I believed that too.

Fast forward 10 or so years later, and I found myself face-to-face with Randy again. I thought I was seeing a ghost when I was at the register ordering food at the local McDonalds near my parents' home when I heard someone calling my name from the drive through window. I only went there because my four year old wanted a Happy Meal. I was on my way to the altar for the second time and was visiting my parents. When I noticed who it was I just waved and smiled. I really wanted to pass out, but I kept cool because of I didn't want my daughter to see my emotions. Later that day he called my parents' phone seven times. He wanted me to cancel my wedding and meet him somewhere. Every word out of his mouth either ended with "…And the Lord" or started with "And the Lord…" I told him that I was glad that he found the Lord, wished him well and proceeded to move forward with my second marriage.

I was about two or three years into my marriage when I got word that Randy had murdered yet another wife. I was puzzled that he was able to get out of jail the first time and I only prayed that he would not be so lucky the second time. This time he received a life sentence. Everyone in my family felt sick to their stomachs. Especially my mom. She knew that on both of those occasions that those two women could have easily been me. One day she admitted that she was glad that she listened to me. I just loved myself too much to not speak up about that situation and my family loved me enough to help protect me. Years after the night of my graduation party, my brother told me that if he would have caught up with Randy that night that he was prepared to go to jail. I know my father felt the same way. Both the men and women in my family carried guns. I'm just glad that they were never used on anyone.

It's been almost 35 years since then. And I've skirted death several times since then. I missed the 1993 World Trade Center bombing because I was on away on business. I used to work on the 63rd floor of that building at that time. I missed 9/11 because I had a new job and was working on Long Island. I often wonder what is so special about my life and why was it spared. I now know that God has some big things in store for me. God has told me that he wants me to positively impact the lives of millions. And I know that as long as I stay on my EDUCATE to ELEVATE mission, I will. With all of the success that I've had in my career and as an author, speaker, and business owner, it's plain to see that I am well on my way. When I look back, I understand that life for me is good. All is well with my husband and two beautiful daughters and I am a living testimony that the past does not equal the future.

FINAL WORDS

We hope that you have enjoyed the stories contained in this book. We believe that they have the ability to change your life. I'm sure that while reading some of the stories you probably thought about your own story. Let's face it, we all have stories where you may have experienced a setback that positioned you for a comeback. We would like to invite you to participate in the next book anthology, "Delayed But Not Denied: Volume 2." If you're interested in becoming a part of our next bestselling book project, please contact us at **www.delayedbutnotdenied.info**

Additionally, you may be interested in your own book anthology project for you and your tribe. If you would like us to assist you with creating a book compilation for you and your peeps contact us. You also might be interested in writing your own book. Either way, you should contact us so we can discuss how we can assist you in making your author dreams come true. You can reach either Toni or Julia by emailing **admin@delayedbutnotdenied.info** or calling us at **646-421-0830** or **917-501-6780**.

Content Curation   Digital Mgmt   Event Asst

Live Social Media   Project Mgmt   SM Strategy + Implement

Traffic Coordinator   Sponsors   Celebrity Brow

$25 $100 (10)   2k or 1k

$100

(logo's
polish)

CPSIA information can be obtained
at www.ICGtesting.com
Printed in the USA
FFOW03n0512201116
29565FF